The Layman's Guide to

True Devotion
to Mary

GW00726107

Dedication

I dedicate my little enterprise to the Immaculate Mary who has been my infallible companion and guide since my childhood. I have no doubt Our Lady will secure for you, as she has for me the secret of happiness - *"Do whatever he tells you."* (Luke 2:5) Mary is truly the cause of my joy, a joy I am eager to share with the entire human family. Without her, even in Heaven, I image my happiness would be incomplete.

A Tribute to Frank Duff

A Commentary on the mystical life of Gods Servant, Frank Duff. Founder of the Legion of Mary

Paul Moran

Frank Duff

Born June 7, 1889,
Founded Legion of Mary, September 7 1921
Died, November 7, 1980

Brunswick
Press
Limited
Est. 1842
design
colour printers
print finishers

Contents   Page

Introduction

Frank Duff is quintessentially THE LAYMAN'S GUIDE TO TRUE DEVOTION TO MARY who lived out his long apostolic life at the highest level of ontological excellence; he put flesh on the words of Jesus: *"I have come so that they may have life and have it to the full."*[1] I apply the words of John Paul II[2] to the life of Frank Duff:

"In every age there have been men and women who, obedient to the Father's call and to the prompting of the Spirit, have chosen this special way of following Christ, in order to devote themselves to him with an "undivided" heart (cf. *1 Cor* 7:34). Like the Apostles, they too have left everything behind in order to be with Christ and to put themselves, as he did, at the service of God and their brothers and sisters. In this way, through the many charisms of spiritual and apostolic life bestowed on them by the Holy Spirit, they have helped to make the mystery and mission of the Church shine forth, and in doing so have contributed to the renewal of society."

His overarching ambition in life was to introduce everyone into a deeper relationship with the Person of the Lord and Saviour Jesus Christ. In keeping with his spirit this little book is entirely driven by that same

---

[1] John 10:10
[2] Vita consecrata – John Paul's post – synodal exhortation to the Church, namely to all those who have consecrated their lives to God and the service of the Gospel

desire by highlighting DeMontfort's True Devotion to Mary that the Servant of God practiced for the greater part of his life; what he referred to as 'The DeMontfort Way.' He maintained "We must so unite ourselves to her that we enter into every aspect of her life, including the higher realm of her mind."[3]

I feel a real sense of relief and satisfaction that I have finally come out of my shell to pay homage to this great man and to put into practise his personal advice to me to begin writing on matters of faith. How quickly time passes; that was in 1976 - I suppose it is never too late to begin! Now I have received a 'thorn in my side' or an unforgiving impulse that urges me to write. In that I have to agree with the Poet, Samuel Lover, "When once the itch of literature comes over a man, nothing can cure it but the scratching of a pen."[4]

What initiated these reflections are the words of Cardinal Leon Joseph Suenens who said **"Frank Duff is a mystic whose intimate spiritual life deserves to be known someday: it will reveal the depth and the source of his achievement and the inspiration."** The Cardinal's words are consonant with the words of Pope John II in his Apostolic Letter Novo Millennio Inuente no 33. "Is it not one of the "signs of the times" that in today's world, despite widespread secularization, there is a widespread

---

[3] Woman of Genesis by Frank Duff Article – Have the mind of Mary
[4] Handy Andy (1842) chapter 36

demand for spirituality, a demand which expresses itself in large part as a renewed need for prayer? Other religions, which are now widely present in ancient Christian lands, offer their own responses to this need, and sometimes they do so in appealing ways. But we who have received the grace of believing in Christ, the revealer of the Father and the Saviour of the world, have a duty to show to what depths the relationship with Christ can lead." It is hoped that my reflections treating of Frank Duff's mystical life will contribute to that end.

I should point out that I have had no formal training in theology nor do I speak with any given authority from the Legion of Mary of which I was a member for over 30 years. My expressed opinions of Francis Michael Duff's spirituality, the Catholic Church, the Legion and De Montfort's 'True devotion to Mary' are my own. The initiative to write this book is entirely my own and the repetitious didactic style is my own; the errors it may contain are mine.

My book is a belated response to a personal invitation from Frank Duff himself. He played a crucial part in my early spiritual development, pointing me in the right direction. It is for the reader to decide if his advice to me to take up writing is well founded or not. In writing about him I am cognisant of Our Saviour's caution, "Man's power is of no use at all," (John 6 – 63) God is not attracted to man's abilities and that He chooses souls for a particular work according to His grace. St. Paul highlights this truth in his letter to the Romans 11: 5 6: "His choice is based on his grace, not on what people do otherwise grace would not be grace." Cognisant of that truth Frank Duff eyed the vast potential of the laity's participation in the Church's apostolate.

I owe him immense gratitude for all he has done for me by way of his talks and writings and graces received through my time in the Legion. I managed to squeeze my thoughts into seven chapters which seem appropriate in that he was born on the 7th June 1889 , the eldest of 7 children; he died at the age of 91 on the 7th of November 1980 and not forgetting that the Legion of Mary held their first meeting on the 7th September 1921. "It came into life with the first fragrance of the Feast of Mary's birthday. It was really born with Mary."[5]

Two people may look upon Frank Duff as he rode his faithful 'Rosinante' – his ancient bicycle-inconspicuously through the Streets of Dublin. One may only see an old man on his way to morning Mass, the other will see one of the bravest, most gallant and awesome Knights of Jesus and Mary in the annuals of the Church. Most passers-by had no idea that he was once the most 'Wanted man' in Communist China with the honorary title "Arch-Imperialist." Unlike Miguel De Cervantes' 'Don Quixote' Frank Duff's dreaming of

---

[5] Frank Duff A Memoir by Father Francis J. Ripley page 4

conquests for his beloved 'Dulcinea' was no fairy tale. He loved Our Lady naturally and supernaturally. Any attempt to study Frank's richly textured spirituality other than using the interpretive lens of True Devotion to Mary would I think lead us down the wrong path. It is my view that the Marian hermeneutic best reveals the mystery of his interior life. As to his apostolic mission we ought not to forget that it was St Louis Marie Grignion DeMontfort or rather his treatise 'True Devotion to Mary' that launched him full sails on his extraordinary mission in the turbulent world of the 20th Century. He echoed the conviction of St Louis Marie DeMontfort who wrote, "They will know what is the surest, the easiest, the shortest and the most perfect means of going to Jesus Christ; and they will give themselves to Mary, body and soul, without reserve, that they may thus belong entirely to Jesus Christ." [6]That in a sense became Frank Duff's life's mission.

The Holy Spirit had given him a founder's Charism; a fiery grain of mustard seed planted in his heart whose divine entelechy would produce a mighty army of lay people namely, the Legion of Mary. Just as St Francis of Assisi pollenated the hearts of men and women centuries before. So too did Francis of Dublin pollinate the hearts of the laity with love for Jesus and Mary, sending them out to establish branches of the Legion into the four corners of the globe. From this perspective I intend to

---

[6] True Devotion 55

make capital by encouraging Catholics to drench themselves in his spirit and seek his powerful intersession and guidance on their journey through life; to reap "the benefits accruing to the Church from his courageous and shining faith". For as Mother Church advises, "When we fix our gaze on the life of men who have followed Christ faithfully, we have a motive that impels us to seek the city that is to come"[7].

As a fervent young Catholic and active member of the Legion of Mary I could only admire him from afar and only in the later years of his life when the high watermark of his holiness became visible for all to see, "love, joy, peace, patient endurance, kindness, generosity, faith, mildness and chastity." (Gal. 5:22, 23) I was one of the large numbers of people who reverently filed pass his open coffin at the Regina Ceoli Hostel and later attended his funeral Mass in Westland Row. The people who gathered around his remains shared one thing in common; they all instinctively revered Frank Duff as a Saint.

In the Legion handbook you will read these words of Cardinal Riberi, formerly Apostolic Delegate to missionary Africa and later Internuncio to China, "The Legion of Mary is apostolic duty decked out in attractive and alluring form; throbbing with life so that it wins all

---

[7] Lumen Gentium 49

to it; undertaken in the manner stipulated by Pope Pius XI, that is, in dependence on the Virgin Mother of God: insistent on quality as the foundation of membership and even as the key to numeral strength; safeguarded by plenteous prayer and self-sacrifice, by the exact system, and by complete co-operation with the priest. The Legion of Mary is a miracle of these modern times."[8]

Mr Duff did not leave a detailed account of his own intimate relationship with God. But he gave us something greater by bequeathing to the Church a blueprint for holiness, namely, the official handbook of the Legion of Mary. Translated in over 80 languages it is an enchiridion on the apostolate of the laity; a compendium of Catholicism in practise. It reveals 'True Devotion to Mary' in practice and demonstrates why the Legion of Mary stands four-square on the principle: "real devotion to the Mother of Jesus obliges apostleship."[9] This is a recurring theme running through his writings. He saw that true love of Mary was inextricably linked with the Saviour's exhortation: *"Go throughout the whole world and preach the gospel to all people."* (Mark 16:15)

As to his own interior disposition we are left somewhat in the dark. However, this has not deterred spiritual writers from attempting to extrapolate from his books

---

[8] H.B. chapter 10 'The Legion Apostolate' section 3
[9] Legion of Mary handbook Chapter 6 section 3 – page31

and voluminous letters the secrets of his mystical life. Happily, there are already a growing number of excellent well researched books and articles written about him readily available. I certainly did not know him in any intimate way as to be capable of rolling away the stone to reveal the inner chamber of his heart. Nevertheless, I share in their eagerness to "behold the man" by making my own contribution. In the process I have discovered that the more I speak about Our Lady the more I understand Frank Duff. Conversely, the more I get to know him the nearer I am drawn into the mystery of the Mother of Jesus. I came to understand what he meant went he said, "If you do not understand Our Lady, you do not understand Christianity."[10]

I take the liberty to borrow the words of St Louis Marie De Montfort to express the overarching ambition of this book. "I feel more than ever inspired to believe and expect the complete fulfilment of the desire that is deeply engraved on my heart and what I have prayed to God for over many years, namely, that in the near or distant future the Blessed Virgin will have more children, servants and slaves of love than ever before and that through them Jesus, my dear Lord, will reign more than ever in the hearts of men."(TD 113)

---

[10] "EVERYBODY MUST POUR HIMSELF INTO ANOTHER SOUL" section 'Without Mary, Jesus is not given.' written by Frank Duff.

I may be guilty of presumption but I feel certain that this brief excursion into the rough terrain of mystical life in general will add to our understanding of the Servant of God, Frank Duff and give the reader a deeper appreciation of the Catholic faith. In particular, the way the Holy Spirit, the Living Flame of Love, dilates, pervades and conquers the human heart through the sweetest intimacy with the Blessed Virgin Mary.

The Author

Laying the Foundation

Chapter 1

"Take it as most certain that you – no matter how unfitted your life may seem for holiness – are being given graces sufficient, if corresponded with, to bring you to sanctity." – Frank Duff

The mystical life of Frank Duff challenges us to open our hearts to God's call to live our lives at the highest level of human existence while living in anticipation of the beatific vision. *"I have come so that they may have life and have it to the full."* (John 10: 10) His life offers us a fascinating insight into the life of a modern Catholic mystic. For this reason I have chosen to examine the transition into higher prayer life that spiritual writers refer to as infused contemplation. I have a feeling Mr Duff is pleased with my method because it has the potential to remind us what he constantly articulated throughout his life, namely, that we are all called to be Saints without exceptions. Indeed, it is for this very reason Mother Church baptises each precious soul, "In the name of the Father, and of the Son, and of the Holy Spirit." Consequently, God calls *"everyone who thirsts, come to the (Holy Spirit) waters; and you that have no money come, buy and eat! Come, buy wine and milk without money and without price."* (Isaiah 55) *"Let everyone who wishes take the water of life as a gift."* (Rev 22:17) That's the 'Good News' Mr Duff celebrated throughout his life and wanted everyone to know that salvation and holiness are indissolubly linked with the Third Person of the Blessed Trinity; that all **life** and holiness comes from the Father, through the Son Jesus Christ **by the working of the Holy Spirit**.[1] Frank Duff ordered his whole life to the working of the Spirit of Love. His magnificent prayer to the Holy Spirit (I will talk about this prayer in another chapter) uniquely unleased the power of the Sacrament of Confirmation among the rank and file of the laity.

The deepest thing in Frank Duff was his commitment to the Holy Spirit

It is hoped that by examining the higher prayer state of contemplation we may easily pick up his trail and follow his footsteps or at least capture the essence of his hidden relationship with the Holy Spirit, "the interior Master of Life according to Christ, a gentle guest and friend who inspires, guides, corrects and strengthens this life." (CCC 1697) We may also begin to experience for ourselves the wonders of a profound relationship with the Holy Spirit without whom there would be no saints. Only cooperation with the Holy Spirit can achieve holiness. Saint John Paul II reminds us "The protagonist is the Holy Spirit who *"Comes to the aid of our weakness."* [2]The Spirit makes it possible for each soul to *"Love the*

---

[1] Eucharistic Prayer III
[2] Crossing the threshold of Hope by John Paul II page 17

Lord your God with all your heart, with all your soul and all your strength." (Deuteronomy 6:5-9 & Luke 10:27) Speaking about Frank Duff, Fr. Bede McGregor, Concilium Spiritual Director of the worldwide Legion of Mary said, "Let there be no mistake the deepest thing in Frank Duff was his commitment to the Holy Spirit."[3] In the Spirit he became apostolically on fire; every fibre of his being was directed towards the corporal and spiritual good of others[4] pouring out his life for the glory of God and the salvation of souls

In preaching the Gospel one is preaching radical freedom

We generally fail to realise that the invitation by the Church to holiness is an invitation to perfect health; one can't imagine any unhealthy people in paradise. Perfect health and ultimate freedom is only found in Jesus Christ. Early in his life Frank discerned the need for personal holiness so as to be rightly ordered to God and neighbour. He saw how it meant freedom in the truest sense of the word. Free to love unconditionally; free to make a gift of ourselves to God; free from the tyranny of rationalism, subjectivism and from all kinds of addiction. Most importantly, free from every form of slavery to Satan. In preaching the Gospel one is essentially preaching radical freedom.

---

[3]Frank Duff and the Legion of Mary by Fr Bede McGregor O.P.
[4] CCC 1766 'To love is to will the good of another'. (St Thomas Aquinas)

Since he took the trouble to write so many inspiring articles, why did he not write a history of his own soul? He may well have thought about it but the whole idea of exposing his intimate relationship with God would be abhorrent to his refined sensibilities. He was indeed full of wisdom, yet he was a humble man.[5] Even though he was an inspirational leader of a world-wide organization, he did not see himself as a paradigm for holiness. Like St. Paul he understood *"Each one of us, however, has been given his own share of grace, given as Christ allotted."* (Ephesians 4:7) Evident by his profound insight into the mystery of the Church as the 'Mystical Body of Christ,' he knew how crucial it was for every Christian to advance in holiness as a necessary condition of every Baptised Christian. That is why Jesus said, *"I am the vine, you are the branches."*[6] Christ is holiness Himself and it stands to reason that all of His members ought to be holy. *"You must be perfect – just as your Father in heaven is perfect."* [7] This instruction from Jesus ought to be framed within the context of an exhortation from a loving Father.

---

[5] See Book 'FRANK DUFF as I knew him' by Father Thomas Flynn C.M. Book pages 62 -63
[6] John 15:5
[7] Matthew 5:48

We know from his life and writings that Mr Duff's reciprocal response to God was to magnify and glorify the Lord, through Mary, in Mary, and with Mary. He wrote in chapter 5 of the handbook: "As it is the pleasure of the Eternal Father so to receive through Mary the homages intended for him, so too he has been graciously pleased to appoint her to be the way by which shall pass to men the various outpourings of his munificent goodness and omnipotence, beginning with the cause of them all - the Second Divine Person made man, our true life, our only salvation." He understood the nature of God is to pour out His goodness upon humanity and that God was pleased to channel His goodness through Mary. Conversely, he knew that everything he gave to God was immeasurably enhanced by channelling everything through her, His chosen Vessel of Honour. Like Jesus Frank Duff became the most obedient son of Mary in order to become the perfect son of the Father. In the same chapter of the handbook you will find this quotation from St Lldephonsus: "If I will make myself dependent on the Mother, it is in order to become the slave of the Son. If I aspire to become her possession, it is in order to render more surely to God the homage of my subjection."

Central to Christianity is man's quest for union with God. *"We love because God loved us first."* (John 1-4:19). Like flowers opening their corollas in response to the warmth of the morning sun, ours is a reciprocal filial response to the Father's paternal love which is poured out upon His children. Through the Son of God entering into human history, (John 3:16) we became God's adopted children; we therefore have the divine right to address Him as 'Abba' (Father). What supreme joy it is to know that we are dearly loved by God and that He is constantly on the quest for each one of us. We are reminded of this whenever we read Paul's second letter to the Christian community at Corinth when he quotes sacred scripture: *"I will make my home with my people and live among them. I will be your father, and you will be my sons and daughters, says the Lord Almighty."* (2 Corinthians 6:16 -18)

The Father and I are one

The thrilling fact is the more we enter into the mystery of Jesus the closer we are drawn to our heavenly Father. According to Pope Benedict XV1 we ought always to: "see Jesus in the light of his communion with the Father, which is the true centre of his personality; without it, we cannot understand him at all, and it is from this centre that he makes himself present to us all today." [8] Jesus

---

[8] Jesus of Nazareth (Book one) foreword page 14 - Bloomsbury

tells us plainly *"The Father and I are one."* (John 10: 30) Earthly life then is in essence a perpetual home coming, if you will, to the eternal embrace of the Father. The touching parabolic image presented to us by Jesus of the Father searching the horizon in anticipation of the return of the prodigal son helps to copper-fasten this eschatological imagery in our minds. Of course, as Christians we acknowledge our 'home coming' is entirely contingent on the Father[9] sending His only Son into the misery of humanity as the only way back to the Father's house.

To see through the window of eternity the reflection of their heavenly Father

Paradoxically, we are the ones who now wait in anticipation for the return of the Son of God. In a sense Jesus is himself the true prodigal Son who squandered his precious Life Blood and returns to the Father blood stained and bearing all our guilt in order to receive on our behalf the Father's embrace and the ring and garment of immortality. *"The Spirit and the Bride say 'Come' ...Come, Lord Jesus"* (Rev 22:17) John Paul II tells us "The Church inspired by the Spirit present in her continues to address this call to the Lord Jesus. She awaits his return."[10] Christians ought to be constantly

---

[9] John 17:3
[10] Homily: Mass for Contemplative Nuns, Hull, Canada September 19th 1984

looking at their crucifixes with unsurpassable gratitude to the figure of the crucified Christ and be able to see in that image the reflection of their heavenly Father holding His outstretched arms, inviting all humanity to run to Him, just as a little child runs into the open embrace of its father. This ought to be the Christian's first contemplative gaze on Truth, namely, recognising the eternal Father in the Person of Jesus Christ. (John 14:9) Jesus tells us plainly, "I am the Way." Thus, He entered into humanity in order for us to enter into His Divinity.

Jesus Christ is not a superstar, Jesus Christ is God

The non-believer would deny Jesus ever existed and the world would make Him out to be a great prophet or holy man. New Agers would make Him out to be a class of superstar but we Christians worship Jesus as God, consubstantial with the Father. I remember when 'Jesus Christ Superstar' was being staged in Dublin for the first time, Frank Duff when asked about the production said "Jesus Christ is not a superstar, Jesus Christ is God." The Bible tells us that Jesus is our Alpha and Omega, our beginning and end. He is the epicentre of human existence. Jesus Christ ought to be the point of orientation of our every thought and action. Jesus is the object of contemplation. (C.C.C. 2724) Jesus is the Absolute who ought to be loved absolutely. Destined for His glory, we ought to reflect Him in our lives and not some hollow projection of ourselves. To shift our gaze from Jesus is tantamount to running ahead of Him; thus exposing ourselves to all sorts of dangers. We do this in countless ways when we consciously or unconsciously impose our own will on Him just as a misguided St. Peter did when he tried to prevent Jesus from going to Jerusalem to fulfil His mission on earth.

The dangers of an egocentric spirituality

One may be surprised how harshly Jesus addressed His beloved Peter, the future head of His Church. However, we ought to realise that Jesus is also addressing Satan who had gained a momentary hold on Peter. It is a sobering thought to realise that even those closest to Jesus can make the fundamental error of following our own rational inclinations. This is a stumbling block best avoided in the spiritual life. Unknowingly we may be developing a unilateral or self-centred relationship with God; a case of us ordering God to our subjective way of thinking instead of objectively ordering our lives to Him and His laws. All of us have at one time or another bargained with God; we say, if you do this for me, I will do such and such for you, kind of attitude. Some individuals would have God pander to their every whim. Frank Duff was aware of the dangers of this egocentric spirituality: [11] He wrote, "Even in its apostolic stage it is possible for one's love to be defective and ones motives

---

[11] Walking with Mary by frank Duff chapter 9 - Now published in the booklet 'Gems of Wisdom' volume 1

flawed. It is more than possible in the non-apostolic members of the Church. It is almost inevitable in the rest of mankind. We may be producing something that looks like loving service of our neighbour, but which may be a hallow sham. It may be only a projection of ourselves. It is possible to be immersed in works of charity and yet to be ministering to ourselves alone. Such self-centred piety is a hideous thing. " He goes on to say: "Thus we make what amounts to idols of ourselves. Virtually we are saying: "I am kind, therefore I must show kindness. I am generous, so I must show generosity. I am patient; I am sweet; I am thoughtful; I am forgiving; I am just; I am merciful – and accordingly I must cause all that loveliness to shine forth from me over the world around me." Plainly that thing is not love, but only as gold – plating on base metal."

Many people believe that they have their desires fixed on God

How often do we come across individuals animated by an unholy impetuosity which they mistake for zeal? They come across as morally self-assured and in full control believing they are individually guided by the Holy Spirit; many of these confuse asceticism with mysticism. One of the tell-tale signs of these religious types is that they find it very hard to bend the knee to lesser authority. They have to be centre stage. Such individuals appear to operate within a whirlwind of activity for the salvation of souls. They are eager to initiate change and they themselves are easily scandalised by the slow pace of others. It would even seem that the gentle Jesus appears to move too slowly for them. It is so easy for well-meaning Christians to slip into this maverick behaviour which is tantamount to self-worship. St. John of the Cross encountered this very problem among the religious of his own day: "Many people believe that they have their desires fixed on God and on spiritual things when in reality they are merely following their own human inclinations." We gather that in the divine scheme of things it is always best to do God's will, rather than pressing forward with our own agenda as excellent as it may be. *"I can do nothing on my own authority; I judge only as God tells me, so my judgement is right, because I am not trying to do what I want, but only what he who sent me wants."* (John 5:30)

Raw on the inside

One cannot help thinking of those T.V. cookery programmes, whereby, the contestants prepare a savoury dish cleverly garnished and well presented on attractive crockery. However, when the judge cuts into the meat, it tells a different story, often the meat is only cooked on the outside and raw on the inside. In the spiritual order, many people consider themselves perfectly cooked on the inside, so to speak, wholly acceptable to the divine palate, however, the opposite may be the reality. To safeguard against self-delusion St Louis Marie de

Montfort strongly advocated consecration to Our Lady in order to allow her to prepare and present our body and soul to God. He knew Our Lady would never allow her devotees to press the cup of sour wine (self-love) to the sacred lips of her Son. De Montfort saw in the Biblical narrative of Rebecca in the book of Genesis (27:1-30)[12] the mystery of Mary's maternal intercession. He understood Rebecca to prefigure Mary, the Mother of God, who carefully prepared and cooked the two kid goats, which represents body and soul that won for her son Jacob, his father Isaac's blessing.

Lead Thou me on

In order to advance in holiness it is necessary that not a stone be left upon a stone, if you will. Therefore the Holy Spirit will have us stand with Mary, the Mother of Jesus at the foot the Cross. There we will experience an earthquake, the sound of thunder and lighting, the earth trembling and rocks splitting apart. Great fissures appear in the ground and buildings fracture and come toppling down. The sanctuary curtain is torn in two, from top to bottom. From top to bottom signifies by the hand of God, and not an act of man. What takes place in the natural order also takes place in the order of grace. The Holy Spirit affects a purifying process or Kenosis - a Greek word which means 'to empty'. Huge cracks begin to appear in our ego, so to speak. The scales fall from

---

[12] True Devotion to Mary 184 to 211

our eyes as the grand image we held of ourselves lies in ruins. Our self-assurance and solid notions of God crumble as the ramparts of self-love are breached allowing grace to rush inwards. In the harsh reality of our dethronement we discover the power of Love ever at work within. Then in humility we ask the Holy Spirit to lead us in the words of Blessed Cardinal John Henry Newman:

> I was not ever thus, nor prayed that thou
> Shouldst lead me on;
> I loved to choose and see my path; but now
> lead thou me on.
> I loved the garish day, and, spite of fears,
> Pride ruled my will: remember not past years.

It is always a healthy sign to see ourselves against the backdrop of 'Infinite Goodness'. In this light, St. Margaret Mary Alacoque like Abraham [13] described herself as mere 'ashes and dust'. Seeing ourselves thus in God's presence we become eager to enthrone Him as Lord of our lives. Not surprising then that the wild Daffodils of humility are to be seen all along the mystical Camino (Way). These yellow springtime flowers herald in the Passion, Death and Resurrection of Our Saviour. Likewise in the order of grace humility ushers in a glorious springtime in which we can truly say with St. Paul as the wick of our ego is removed, "*It is not*

---

[13] Genesis 18: 20 -22

I who live, but Christ who lives in me." (Gal 2:20) Writing about Frank Duff, Cardinal Suenens made this telling observation: "We find in the handbook a marked insistence on humility as an indispensable and primary quality in a legionary."[14] In fact before business gets underway the rosary is recited at every Legion meeting and the Legionaries praise the name of "Jesus" and equally acknowledge their disposition before Him 50 times when they say "Holy Mary Mother of God, pray for us sinners now and at the hour of our death amen." Mr Duff knew that God meets humanity beneath the falls of Merciful Love and that He will not deal with those who elevate themselves above the falls, in other words *"God opposes the proud, but gives grace to the humble."*[15]

No two souls are exactly alike

The Doctor of the Church, St. Therese of the Child Jesus said, "I realise for the most part not all souls have the same battles, yet no two souls are exactly alike." Truly the Holy Spirit is not restricted to any particular modality in His dealings with souls. When reading the lives of the saints one is amazed at the wonderful way the Holy Spirit works in their lives. Nevertheless, according to the Carmelite Masters there are certain experiences which are normal to one growing in union with Christ. In the next chapter I will attempt to

---

[14] Frank Duff Pioneer of the New Evangelization, page 76
[15] James 4:6

highlight some of these contemplative experiences. However, before examining them it is best to highlight the paramount importance of the virtue of humility. The saints are in agreement, it is the virtue of humility that orders us to God. Consequently, as we advance into the higher stages of spiritual life we are obliged to take the words of Jesus seriously, *"Learn of me because I am meek and humble of heart."*

To stoop down to our littleness in order to raise us up to Himself

Soon the yellow daffodil is nowhere to be seen. A new flower appears upon the vernal landscape of the soul. The little daisy of nothingness makes its appearance, that is to say, the virtue of humility evanesces into a deeper and more refined sense of our own worth before Almighty God. Contrary to the ways of the world which tend to journey upwards towards greatness and notoriety, the Holy Spirit directs souls downwards into the abyss of one's own nothingness. Nothingness is a dynamic word in the vocabulary of the Carmelites mystics. The virtue of nothingness becomes deeply rooted in the individual after we have been caught like the wild stallion, harnessed, broken, and saddled. Here we touch upon the very heart of John of the cross's 'Nada' (nothing) theology. For St Therese the virtue of nothingness blossomed into her 'Little Way' of spiritual childhood which she understood to have the power to compel Almighty God to stoop down to our littleness in order to raise us up to Himself. She wrote, "In order that Love may be satisfied it must needs stoop to very nothingness and transform that nothing into fire."[16]

Let me know myself, Lord, and I shall know you

St Therese who was herself a spiritual daughter of John of the cross and Teresa of Avila said "It is sufficient to recognise one's nothingness and to abandon oneself as a child into God's arms." Another great Doctor of the Church St. Augustine had this to say: "Let me know myself, Lord, and I shall know you." Blessed Angela de Foligno sings from the same hymnbook when she said. "To know the all-ness of God and the nothing-ness of man – that is perfection". Emphasising this point John Paul II quotes the well-known words Christ addressed to St Catherine of Siena "He (God) who is" and "She (individual) who is not"[17] To the subjective mindset all this talk of humility will appear rather negative. However one ought not to be put off because in due time we will discover an amazing sense of inner freedom tantamount to setting free the 'wounded child' within all of us, so to speak, in order to become a healthy child of God. This was St Therese's great discovery. In fact she discovered a secret that God never intended to be a secret.

---

[16] STORY OF A SOUL, CH X1
[17] Crossing the threshold of Hope by John Paul II page 38

Frank Duff saw with his contemplative gaze that walking with Mary lead him away from the dangers of mere asceticism to the path of mysticism. He saw too the complementarity of spiritual childhood and Mary's spiritual motherhood. I think it is fair to say that he looked upon 'walking with Mary' (union with Mary) as the best spiritual exercise that a Christian could do to become a healthy person. He reaped the benefits of a true and tender love for Our Lady and he wanted to share his 'Secret of Mary' with everybody. He knew Mary wants what's best for her children, namely, to receive all the graces that flow from the Sacred Heart of her Son, Jesus Christ.

The humbler you are the happier you shall be

St Therese couldn't state it any plainer: "The humbler you are the happier you shall be." St Therese had that childlike trust and audacity to appear before her heavenly Father empty handed. I imagine if one was to dust down the interior life of Frank Duff, so to speak, one will discover the fingerprints of St Therese of the Child Jesus on the flat surfaces of his Marian spirituality. Frank Duff's childlike love for Mary was a reflection of his love for God the Father. I mention this because in my opinion Therese of Lisieux is an important link in understanding DeMontfort's true devotion to the Blessed Virgin Mary. Elsewhere I will discuss the synergism between spiritual childhood and devotion to Mary and examine the influence of St Therese on the early life of the founder of the Legion of Mary.

The Spirit of Love sets me aflame with his fire

The Mother of Jesus is the greatest mystic that lived on earth; she personified the virtue of nothingness. It logically follows that those who have an intimacy of union with her will automatically be lead along the same path. How wonderful! Just as Our Lady was present on Calvary at the death of her Son on the Cross, so too she is present at our mystical death from the world; in nothingness we are reborn in God. Was it not in the womb of Mary's nothingness that the Holy Spirit created His unsurpassable masterpiece, namely, Jesus Our Lord. In Mary Jesus was born in nothingness! So too, in the Immaculate Heart of Mary the Holy Spirit will hover over the dark waters of our nothingness and recreate us in Jesus Christ. In this poverty of detachment from all created things devoid of power and human wisdom the Living Flame of Love burns sweetly within our hearts gently transforming us into living images of Jesus Christ. In that sense it is the Catholic mystic who understands that the *'New Jerusalem'* comes down with the same power that created the universe and dwells in the temple of our hearts. It is in Mary that you will come to discover God's unique speciality, namely, to create and recreate from nothingness. *"By the word of the Lord, the heavens were made, and all their host by the breath of his mouth.*" (Psalm 33:6)

The agony and ecstasy of earthly life

One thing is certain that when the transforming fire of Trinitarian Love penetrates the deepest recesses of the soul the individual is apt to feel an interior restlessness. I am not saying one will be miserable for the rest of their lives. What I am saying is that the atmosphere within the souls undergoes a perceptible change and from this time onwards a holy restlessness mischievously tinkers with one's day to day existence. One will have to come to terms with the agony and ecstasy of mystical life until one passes through the valley of death; then one will only have to contend with ecstasy. The reason for this is that unlike all things created this non-contingent flame of Love cannot be exhausted as it emanates from the heart of the Blessed Trinity. Joy accompanies this eternal flame because it has within it the anticipation of eternal glory. St Therese acknowledged this reality when she wrote: "The Spirit of Love sets me aflame with his fire. You put this Fire of Heaven in my soul. And the fire of love which consumes my soul – shall never go out."

I came to set the earth on fire

Perhaps this may explain why Catholics advanced in grace have such a strong affiliation with the suffering souls in Purgatory. Even though one is assuaged with indescribable joy both suffer in their spirit the pain of longing for God. From the writings of the St. John of the Cross we know that the Holy Spirit adopts a scorched earth policy, if you will, creating a veritable 'Terra Del Fuego' (land of fire) upon Sodom and Gomorrah, that is to say, upon sense and spirit. The scorching breath of the Holy Spirit passes through the very marrow of our bones. John having experienced this himself describes this purifying fire as the 'The Dark Night of the Soul' a poetic euphemism for the painful regeneration and transformation that must take place in the lives of all those advancing in grace and the knowledge of God. This Spanish mystic reminds those under his spiritual direction, *"The Lord your God is a devouring fire."* (Deuteronomy 4:24) Jesus said: *"I came to set the earth on fire."* (Luke 12:49) Not surprising in describing their relationship with God mystics often make reference to fire. In fact all three Carmelite mystics, John of the cross, Teresa of Avila and Therese of Lisieux give us graphic accounts of having been assaulted by fire.[18]

The Holy Trinity deals with us only through the Holy Spirit

Like all great Catholic teachers Frank Duff knew that submission to the Holy Spirit is the key ingredient for living out our Christian vocation. In a private letter to Cardinal Suenens he wrote: "Nor must we forget that the Holy Trinity deals with us only through the Holy Spirit."

---

[18] Transverberation or Wound of Love

Furthermore, he made that vital connection between the work of the Holy Spirit and Our Lady. On page 53 of the handbook of the Legion of Mary you will come across this statement: "The sole purpose of Mary's existence is to conceive and bring forth the whole Christ, that is the Mystical Body with all its members perfect, and fitly joined together (Ephesians 4:16), and with its Head, Jesus Christ." "Mary accomplishes this in co-operation with, and by the power of the Holy Spirit, who is the life and soul of the Mystical Body. It is in her bosom and subject to her maternal care that the soul grows up in Christ and comes to the age of His fullness."

Let us run together

Over the course of many years Frank Duff enlightened many 20th century Catholics to take up the practise of True devotion to Mary. Basically there are just two kinds of relationships with Our Lady, one perfect and the other not so perfect. In the past many great saints walked with Mary. However, I use the metaphor of running with Mary to connote the higher degree of union with her, that is to say, the perfect relationship of intimacy that Jesus has with His Mother. In Frank Duff's case I find this passage of sacred scripture particularly appropriate: *"Draw me in your footsteps, Let us run together."* (Song of Songs 1:14) We can say without fear of contradiction that he ran with Mary. It goes without saying that he started out walking with Mary in order to run with her.

Now all this may be a little too much to take in at once. Don't worry, as you go from chapter to chapter things will become a lot clearer to you.

Our Lady teaches us the science of the Holy Spirit

Frank Duff was fully aware "Our Lady teaches us the science of the Holy Spirit with the result that we are found to be attentive to the One who is the Unknown Paraclete."[19] Thus, from this perspective he penned one of the most powerful prayers ever written in the Catholic Church, namely, the Legion Promise: "I know that you, (Holy Spirit) who have come to regenerate the world in Jesus Christ, have not willed to do so except through Mary......."[20]

All the faithful are invited and obliged to holiness and the perfection of their own state in life

John Paul II tells us "Christian mysticism is born of the Revelation of the living God. This God opens Himself to union with man, arousing in him the capacity to be united with Him, especially by means of the theological virtues of faith, hope, and, above all, love."[21] Fr. Marie Eugene of the Child Jesus, a Carmelite mystic tells us, "Every soul possessing the seven gifts received at baptism can be moved by God and brought by Him to

---

[19] Frank Duff Pioneer of the New Evangelization - Suenens
[20] The Legion handbook Chapter 15 page 90/91
[21] Crossing the threshold of hope by John Paul II page 88

the plenitude of the mystical life, including supernatural contemplation." [22]   Vatican II is of the same frame of mind: "All Christians in any state or walk of life are called to the fullness of Christian life and to the perfection of love....All the faithful are invited and obliged to holiness and the perfection of their own state in life[23]." (Lumen Gentium 40, 42)

Infinite possibilities await ordinary laypeople

Before the formation of the Legion of Mary and long before Vatican II, Frank Duff wrote in his first publication: "Take it as most certain that you – no matter how unfitted your life may seem for holiness – are being given graces sufficient, if corresponded with, to bring you to sanctity." [24]   That truth fused in his conscientiousness and allowed him to believe that by virtue of one's baptism into the life of Christ infinite possibilities awaited the ordinary layperson.

---

[22] I want to see God, by Fr. Marie Eugene O.C.D. Chapter IIIV page 477
[23] HB chapter 33 section 13
[24] Can we be Saints? By Frank Duff

The Divine Invasion

Thirst for God is quenched by the waters of eternal life.[1]

Nothing has ever surpassed the allegorical imagery of the caterpillar metamorphosing into a butterfly presented to us by the great Spanish Doctor of mystical science St Teresa of Avila representative of a soul advancing into the mystical olive grove of infused contemplation. In this chapter I am going to briefly sketch the transition into the contemplative experience of those we describe as contemplatives or mystics. This way we may gain fresh understanding of Frank Duff's faith based hyperawareness of God and Our Lady in his life. Perhaps it will allow us to see through the same interpretive lens as he did. In order for me to do this I will draw inspiration from the springs of the great Carmelite Teachers, Mystics and Doctors of the Church.

As silver is purified by fire so you have tested us.

One's first reading of the writings of St. John of the Cross fills one with a curiosity to know more about

---

[1] Catechism of the Catholic Church 2557

advanced life in the Spirit. However, it won't be long before one comes to the stark conclusion that the contemplative experience, whether active in the world or behind the cloisters, is no bed of roses. When the Holy Spirit initiates a soul into a higher level of prayer life, namely, 'infused contemplation,' He places a seal upon the heart so to speak that He may take full possession of that person. (Cant/Song of Songs 8:6) When this happens one may expect to experience the full rigors of being held by the Holy Spirit. I think that every saint/mystic would agree with the Psalmist: *You have put us to the test, God; as silver is purified by fire so you have tested us."* (Psalm 66) At this stage it is necessary to explode the myth, namely, that mystics retreat from the world and people in order to be alone with God; the opposite is the reality, mystics are intensely apostolic. Frank Duff saw the world as the place where man encounters God and he engaged it just as the Apostles and the early Christians did 2000 years ago.

Take the bitter with the sweet

As stressed in the previous chapter, to advance in grace one's self-autonomy has to be crushed in the winepress of Gethsemane. This has to be so if we are to be absorbed into the Divine Will. To the contemporary subjective mindset that may sound unreasonably harsh and even destructive to one's personality. However, seen from the panopticon of the transforming union nothing could be further from the truth. Human happiness has its epicentre in the will of God. There are many degrees of happiness that an individual may achieve in life. However the type of happiness we are treating here cannot be achieved entirely by one's own efforts. By our own efforts we may reach a certain state of enlightenment or Nirvana but as far as Christianity is concerned that is only a beginning. True happiness does not come from enlightenment but from total surrender of one's life to the will of God. On earth Jesus only desired the fulfilment of the Father's will. Why should it be any different for His followers? John of the Cross points out, "In the state of divine union a person's will is to be completely transformed into God's will that it excludes everything contrary to God's will, and in all and through all is motivated by the will of God." St Teresa of Avila offers her own encouraging words: "The highest perfection consists not in interior favours or in great raptures or in visions or in the spirit of prophecy, but in the bringing of our wills so closely into conformity with the will of God that, as soon as we realise that He wills anything, we desire it ourselves with all our might, and take the bitter with the sweet, knowing that to be His Majesty's will."

What a terrible thing it is to fall into the hands of the living God

John of the Cross paints a rather haunting image of a soul advancing in grace through what he calls the purifying dark night of the soul. Add to that the voice of other saints such as St. Margaret Mary Alacoque who exclaimed, "Oh! What a terrible thing it is to fall into the hands of the living God".[2] One doubts whether Margaret Mary realised that she was actually quoting sacred scripture (Hebrews 10:31) in making this statement. Teresa of Avila echoes the same sentiments, "Oh, God bless me, Lord! How cruel thou art to thy lovers!" (Chapter X1 - The Interior Castle) Nevertheless, far from being put off or even comprehending the wisdom of John's mystical theology, one becomes strangely attracted to this Spanish priest who was so utterly in love with his Creator.

The desire for God is a preparation for union with God

In his writings John of the Cross addresses the hunger for God that lies secretly or consciously in the heart of every human being. One cannot passionately desire something that does not exist in the first place. Who in their right mind does not want to grow in love with God? Why would anyone "prefer to reign in hell, than serve in heaven" as if you could reign in hell. John of the cross maintained "The desire for God is a preparation for union with God." (Stanza III 'Living Flame of Love') One is at ease in the company of this great Carmelite reformer who contemplated the grandeur of the human person bathed in God's glory. St. Therese of the Child

---

[2] The Autobiography of Saint Margaret Mary – section 99

Jesus described him to Sr. Marie of the Trinity, "He is the saint of Love par excellence." St. Teresa of Avila was so impressed with his intelligence and his elevated union with God that she said to a fellow prioress, "Give thanks to God for having ordained that you shall have Father John so near you...I have not found another like him in the whole of Castile, nor anyone who inspires souls with such fervour to journey to heaven." Equally, her words could well have been said about Frank Duff.

Assimilation into the Light of God

Like Madre Teresa John's particular charism allowed him to describe in depth the various nuances of passing shade during the soul's assimilation into the Light of God; from the earthbound myopic caterpillar to the ultra violet gaze of the free flying butterfly. Paradoxically, we journey in darkness, that is to say, by faith, as a prelude to living in perpetual Light. For as scripture says: *"The gates of the city will stand open all day; they will never be closed because there will be no night there."* (Rev. 21: 25) In dealing with matters of life in the Spirit, St John of the Cross speaks with admiral authority as one who has penetrated the Transcendent Absolute and discovered within his own mortal frame the pulse of Trinitarian life. Guided by the 'Living Flame of Love' who burned deeply in his breast, he walked through dark valleys (trails of faith), and braved the terrible fire storms (the purgation of sense and spirit) while maintaining the anxious holding patterns (the dire longing for God and the yearning to be released from the bondage of earthly life) on his spiritual flight to God. In other words he has come through the great tribulation whereby the fires of Substantial Love have passed through all his faculties, even burning away the barrier to his sub consciousness. There John catches Love in the very act of loving within him.

I die, because I do not die

Not surprising his writings vibrate with celestial joy and holy unction as he presses the boundaries of human expression to reach out beyond the substance of clay/matter to remind a doubtful world that *"God loved the world so much that he gave his only Son, so that everyone who believes in him may not die but have eternal life".(John 3:16)* Accordingly, John of the Cross saw the primacy of love in all things and he maintained that "death is naught else than the privation of life for when life comes, there remains no trace of death." (Stanza II – 28 Living Flame of Love)

Life is a gift, and I intend to live it as long as I can

My father said to me three weeks before his death; "Life is a gift, and I intend to live it as long as I can." A few days later, having fallen out of bed I found him unconscious, he ended up in intensive care in hospital. I visited him every day in hospital and observed that, true to his word, he indomitably fought for life every step of the way before his heart failed. He was 87 years of age. My father was right, life is a wonderful gift and ought to be lived to the full. Nevertheless, the Catholic mystic is one who having been wounded by Love at a certain point in his or her life is entirely congruent with the mindset of John of the Cross when he issued that famous paradoxical statement, "I die, because I do not die." John's state of soul may be compared to a tethered little puppy straining and pining with unbridled eagerness in anticipation of the Masters return. He speaks on behalf of all those ordinary people who have 'found what they were looking for' in life and consequently burn with unbridled longing for God. This longing becomes an open wound in the heart of the Christian mystic; a stigmata that no earthly medicine can cure.

Death, will bring more

Particularly in his later years Frank Duff would have lived within this mystical inner tension that St Paul also mentioned, *"For what is life? To me it is Christ, Death, will bring more. But if by continuing to live I can do more worthwhile work, then I am not sure which I should choose. I am pulled in two directions. I want very much to leave this life and be with Christ, which is a far better thing; but for your sake it is much more important that I remain alive."* (Philippians 1:21-24) No human being endured this inner martyrdom more than the

Blessed Virgin Mary, who after the Ascension of her Son had to endure that acute separation for the rest of her earthly life. We constantly seek visible signs of the extraordinary in the lives of saintly people; I am not implying that there is any harm in that. However, what we generally fail to understand is that like the early morning mist that shrouds the undulations and rich greenery of the land, the interior life of the mystic is for the most part cloaked in simplicity.

His camouflage was not entirely of his own making

It is not easy to detect this mystical condition in any individual. One may live life to the full and yet suffer a gnawing desire to be with Jesus and Mary in heaven. This spiritual 'sickness of love' can easily be disguised and I firmly believe that to be the case with Mr Duff. Behind his gracious smile and outgoing personality, not to mention his crushing workload, his heart burned in restless torment for the Face of God he so dearly loved. However, as is the case with the interior life of Our Lady his camouflage was not entirely of his own making, but assisted by the Holy Spirit, as Psalm 31:20 states: *"Safe in your presence you hide them, far from human plotting, shielding them in your tent, far from contentious tongues"*.[3]

---

[3] See Living Flame of Love – John of the Cross - stanza 2 verse 17

Frank Duff was well acquainted with the purgative and redemptive aspect of the work of the Holy Spirit who draws souls into the perfection of Christ and makes them collaborators in His Redemptive mission. The Spirit makes it possible for each soul to *"Love the Lord your God with all your heart, with all your soul and all your strength."* (Deuteronomy 6:5-9 & Luke 10:27) Like St. Bernadette of Lourdes the soul cries out "My God, I love you with all my heart, all my soul, all my strength." [4] It is clear from the following passage that Frank Duff understood the manifold meaning of suffering, he wrote: "Suffering is always a grace. When it is not to bestow healing, it is to confer power. It is never merely a punishment for sin. "Understand", says St. Augustine, "that the affliction of Mankind is no penal law, for suffering is medicinal in its character." And on the other hand, the passion of our Lord overflows as an inestimable privilege, into the bodies of the sinless and the saintly in order to conform them ever more perfectly to his own likeness." [5]

He makes me dwell in darkness

In the contemplative state, one is blinded by the Light, if you will. Imagine if someone held a powerful torchlight

---

[4] Bernadette Speaks by Fr. Rene Laurentin - page 530
[5] Legion handbook chapter 9

in front of our eyes, although we are suffused in light, nevertheless, we are plunged into darkness, hence the expression, "Faith is darkness to the understanding." (St. Dionysius) According to John of the Cross the nearer to God we get the greater the demand of faith. He unambiguously stressed the paramount importance of faith. In stanza 12 of his spiritual canticle he writes: "Indeed, there is no other means by which one reaches true union and spiritual espousal with God, as Hosea indicates *"I will espouse you to me in faith."*" (Hosea 2:20) It is wrong to assume that mystics are constantly entering in and out of ecstatic states, having visions and the likes. The opposite is generally the reality, as Psalm 143: 3 says, *"He makes me dwell in darkness."* Every Christian is required to master the art of living by faith alone. *"Do you believe because you see me? How blessed are those who believe without seeing me!"* (John 20:29)

Be firm in faith

In the shadow play of human existence it is faith that enlightens human reason: faith is a type of rainbow bridging heaven with earth. Pope John Paul II suggests this when he said, "Be firm in faith! Faith spans for us the infinite spaces of transcendence, makes us bow our heads before God, and unites us intimately with Jesus

Christ, true God and true man."[6] John of the Cross insists, "The understanding must withdraw from itself, and walk in faith, believing and not understanding. And in this way the understanding will reach perfection. For by faith and by no other means comes union with God; and the soul approaches God more nearly by not understanding than by understanding." (Stanza III - 48 Living Flame of Love)

My God, I believe, I adore, I hope, and I love You

At Fatima the Angel was sent to stir the baptismal waters of Faith, Hope and Charity within the little children in order to prepare them for sainthood and to strengthen them for the mission that God had called them to carry out. The Angel gave them a prayer: "My God, I believe, I adore, I hope, and I love You. I ask forgiveness for those who do not believe, nor adore, nor hope nor love you………." One simply cannot overstate the importance of the Angel's prayer. It tapped into the power supply of baptismal grace and won for the three illiterate children the admiration of the world. The French Carmelite mystic Fr. Marie-Eugene makes this important point in regards the power of baptismal grace, "Therese (of the Child Jesus) was indeed a great mystic and a great contemplative, but she was so because of her baptismal grace. We should not relegate contemplation

[6] 'Day by Day with Pope John Paul' page 30 – Paulist Press New York /Ramsey

to mythical, inaccessible regions, but rather give it its true role as the development of our baptismal grace."[7] Frank Duff was well aware of this reality.

The 'salt of the earth' loses its taste

Living by faith means we do not always have to know the reason for the Holy Spirit's action in our lives. St John of the Cross tells us that "In this dark night of faith God enters the soul and purifies it from ignorant thoughts and imperfections, whether they are continuous, natural or spiritual. The contemplatives call this infused contemplation or mystical theology. This is where God teaches the soul in secret and instructs it in perfect love, while the soul does nothing and understands nothing about this infused contemplation." At a time of His choosing, the Holy Spirit opens the flood gates to contemplation. Allegorically speaking, as this dark water converges with the white water of earthly living 'the salt of the earth' loses its taste, that is to say, we begin to hunger more and more for the things of heaven rather than the things of earth. Interiorly this effect is acutely felt within our faculties and John provides a sound reason for it: "This corruptible human life is incompatible with the other incorruptible life of God". (The Spiritual Canticle stanza 11 p512)

---

[7] Under the Torrent of His Love – page 36 (Alba House – New York)

Shock waves begin to register in one's consciousness as one enters the contemplative state whereby the pattern of prayer life changes quite dramatically. Let me explain by way of analogy. Imagine that you have become accustomed to living in an amazon forest type environment and the constant daily round of plodding your way through dense undergrowth. You have become completely acclimatised to the enclosed environment whereby one treads slowly cutting away a path with the aid of a machete; the machete being an essential tool. Then one day a dramatic change takes place as the play of light shafting through the leafy canopy appears brighter and brighter. As you advance towards the sunlight you abruptly come to the edge of the forest. Suddenly, stretching as far as the eye can see there is a vast arid landscape with not even a tree in sight! A new environment beckons. Similarly, as one is drawn by the Spirit into the higher state of supernatural contemplation, a climate change takes place within the interior of the soul. At this stage one may say that the 'Divine Invasion' has begun.

Into the harsh arid desert environment

Like St. Paul after his Damascus experience, the Holy Spirit directs souls into the desert. Metaphorically speaking they are lead away from the humid forest environment with all its rich moist earthy smells and fragrances, which is representative of sense and into the harsh arid desert environment which represents the way of the Spirit. All seems well at first. Freed from the constraints of the confined forest environment one is overtaken with an initial feeling of euphoria; the individual cannot fail to notice this dramatic change. In this vast wilderness there is nothing to restrict or slow one down, one is completely free to run, jump, and dance like David before the Ark of the Covenant, as it were. However, all is premature. Slowly the harsh breezes of aridity begin to penetrate the recesses of the soul thereby imposing a new set of limitations.

Pillars of salt

If ever there was a warning light to flash, it is here at this bifurcation of sense and Spirit. St John of the cross warns that Satan stands at this fork in the road to prevent us from entering into the contemplative state, the way of the spirit. Unfortunately, at this stage many individuals baulk and become unsettled and seek to return to the familiar forest atmosphere or comfort zone of sense experience, thereby seeking to regain their autonomy and interior equilibrium. As the Spirit begins to rain down fire of his choosing, it is crucial not to turn around or look back. To do so is to run the risk of turning into 'pillars of salt',[8] or to put it another way, it is tantamount

---

[8] The Book of Genesis chapter 19

to breaking free of the cocoon and crawling back to caterpillar status. How awful! Only by pressing forward boldly in faith do we surrender control to the Holy Spirit and abandon ourselves to Divine Providence. This way the Spirit is free to refine the theological virtues of Faith, Hope and Love – especially Faith. These theological virtues are the higher gifts that St. Paul speaks about. They are the massive columns that support the superstructure of life in the Spirit. Without these gifts one cannot know or possess the Transcendent God.

I can't pray anymore

Almost immediately we notice other subtle changes in our prayer life. This is because the first green shoots of contemplation are now beginning to germinate. Gradually the individual loses the ability to meditate and vocal prayer now becomes an ordeal. One regularly hears people say, "I can't pray anymore." This is because, metaphorically speaking, in the hot treeless desert of contemplation the 'machete' of vocal prayer is no longer a requirement since there are no branches to be cut. St. John of the Cross indicates that it is detrimental to engage in vocal prayer during the time the Holy Spirit is secretly drawing the soul into interior solitude. In this interior solitude the individual experiences supernatural peace which engenders a deeper sense of prayer. As the Psalmist says, *"He lets me rest in fields of green and leads me to quiet pools of fresh water. He gives me new strength.[9]*" It is a wonderful thing to experience what Jesus Himself experienced, namely, the compulsion to seek out quiet places to commune with the Eternal Father. I believe that Frank Duff's experienced this 'green pasture' quietly praying his breviary in the presence of his Lord in the Blessed Sacrament; there he received new strength to stoically meet every challenge.

Vocal prayer

Initially, the touch of the Holy Spirit will register perceptibly in regards to vocal prayer. He literally renders the individual speechless! When this happens, individuals will not be able to vocalise their thoughts or aspirations while He acts within them. This may happen when one is engaged in praying the Rosary or other vocal prayers. Quite suddenly one becomes aware of strange stirrings within the heart area. Immediately there is a dramatic loss of breath. In seconds, they are overcome by the power of the Spirit and no matter how hard they try; they cannot utter a single word! St Teresa of Avila mentions this touch of the Holy Spirit in her book 'Interior Castle': "When the Spouse wishes to ravish a soul, he commands that the doors of the mansions be closed ...Breath leaves the body, it is impossible to speak." Initially, there may be moments of panic in the struggle to gather breath. However, there is no real danger of not being able to breathe; it is just that

---

[9] Psalm 23 verse 2:3

the Spirit has momentarily suspended the faculty of speech. During this phenomenon the heart beats irregularly, the eyes naturally close as the head dips forward and the body maintains the ability to support its own weight. Although held in blissful suspension, individuals generally remain in touch with their surroundings. This ravishment of the heart may only last a few minutes, before speech returns. Thus, by such sugar coated methods the Holy Spirit weans certain individuals off vocal prayer.

The Spirit has pressed the pause button

For others there may be no inner feelings just the sensation of having lost the ability to engage in vocal prayer; the Spirit has pressed the pause button, so to speak. St. Margaret Mary describes her own experience of this phenomenon in her Autobiography: "As this Sovereign Lord of my soul pursued me so closely regardless of time and place. I was unable to pray vocally and although I did violence to myself in order to do so, I nevertheless remained sometimes without being able to pronounce a single word, especially when reciting the rosary." Margaret Mary expressed the encouragement of Jesus in regards to her inability to recite vocal prayers. "He replied that I was not to force myself any more to say vocal prayers, but to be satisfied with what was of obligation, adding thereto the Rosary when I was able." [10] Even St Therese who had a great love for Our Lady and her rosary experienced difficulty with vocal prayer. Therese told her sister: "The recitation of the Rosary is more difficult for me than the wearing of an instrument of penance. I feel I have said it so poorly! I force myself in vain to meditate on the mysteries of the rosary." [11] After a short period individuals instinctively discern when to remain silent and when to pray vocally. St. John of the Cross is by no means saying that when individuals arrive at the contemplative state, they automatically cease to pray vocally, especially the Lord's Prayer or the Hail Mary. It is really a matter of how each individual copes with the pressing need for interior silence whereby the voice of the Divine Guest gently calls *"Come and worship me."* [12]

Speak Lord, for your servant is listening

In peaceful interior silence we emit a non-vocal appeal – *"Speak Lord, for your servant is listening."* (1 Samuel 3:10) It also says in the book of Job *"be silent and I will teach you wisdom."* (Job 33-33) Rather than a deliberate act of raising the mind and heart to God one becomes instinctively aware of God's presence: *"I know that your goodness and love will be with me all my life; and your house will be my home as long as I live."* [13] One becomes

---

[10] Autobiography of St. Margaret Mary Alacoque section 81
[11] The story of a Soul – Chapter 11
[12] Psalm 27 verse 8
[13] Psalm 23 verse 6

absorbed in this awareness of God's presence within and adapts to praying without words, images and thoughts. Even going to sleep seems so different; in a sense one no longer falls asleep, rather, one evanesces into a state of peaceful oblivion. On occasions it will take all one's efforts to stave off a peaceful heaviness in order to stay awake during the day; even during Mass. Other strange phenomena may also occur to indicate the presence of the Holy Spirit. Perhaps one of the strangest is flights of spirit. One may suddenly experience oneself flying silently at speed over unknown territory or flouting in an unknown weightless dimension; flights or transports of the spirit are apt names for this phenomenon. These and other strange inward manifestations are derived from the fact that one has become drenched to the inner depths of ones being with the presence of the Holy Spirit. In this light it is easier to understand the phenomenon of levitation and bilocation; one's spirit is raised to God and human nature is inclined to simulate these vibrations.

Meditation

Now we come to the prayer of mediation. John of the Cross tells us: "The soul now finds that its own spirit no longer needs the effort of meditation; it enjoys loving contemplation."[14] It appears the Holy Spirit uses similar tactics as those of vocal prayer, although less dramatic.

---

[14] The Dark night of the soul – Book 2 section 1

The Holy Spirit causes a drought upon the faculty of imagination causing the tributaries of imagery to dry up completely. So now the soul has lost the ability to meditate. Consequently, individuals no longer have the power to gather the pixels of imagery within the faculty of their imagination. It really is astonishing how one day a person can manufacture beautiful vivid Technicolor images in their minds eye of biblical scenes and in no time, there is only a blank screen. The Holy Spirit has pulled the plug and all channels are lost, if you will. The direct result of this is that the door to the natural acts of meditation is firmly shut and all nuances of spiritual sweetness evaporate leaving the soul in a state of spiritual dryness. In this state of aridity the soul is being prepared to soak up God just as a dry sponge will do if it is immersed in water. Likewise, by means of spiritual dryness the Holy Spirit lovingly draws souls into the deep silent waters of contemplation, the state of 'pure receiving,' as John of the Cross describes contemplation.

We have only this life to practise the virtue of faith

For individuals the onset of 'dryness in prayer' can be somewhat bewildering. Another great mystic, St Paul of the Cross, founder of the Passionist Order gives valuable advice and encouragement to those who find themselves in this situation: "Do not be disturbed by the obscurity in which you find yourself. These trials are necessary for you to exercise your faith, so that deprived of every image you remain steadfast in that interior solitude, resting in God and worshipping him in spirit and in truth." St Therese of the Child Jesus also saw the positive side of spiritual dryness: "It is so sweet to serve Our Lord in the night of trial; we have only this life to practise the virtue of faith!" However, the trial of faith is by no means the only thing the fledgling contemplative has to deal with. It is at this stage that the incurable sickness of love manifests itself.

The torment that dominates the mystical way

One recalls a brilliant young German philosopher and self - confessed atheist, Edith Stein, who on finding herself alone one evening in a friend's house picked out a copy of the 'Autobiography of St Teresa of Avila' to pass the time. Edith became immediately captivated by the interior life of this Spanish mystic as Teresa's writings formed a nexus with her intellectual work as a Phenomenologist. She becomes excited and avidly reads throughout the night. The dawn comes and correspondently Truth dawns on the young Edith who having finished the book exclaims with an air of triumph, "Here is Truth!" Today we honour her as St. Teresa Benedicta of the Cross[15]a Carmelite. After her conversion she rapidly became a Catholic mystic. Edith situates the phenomenon of the 'sickness of love' within the context of the Dark Night of the soul. She explains,

---

[15] Feast day is celebrated on the 9th August

"The ardent desire for the hidden God seems to be, as it were, the torment that dominates the whole mystical way. It does not even cease in the bliss of the (transforming union) bridal union. It adds to it, in a certain sense, through the growing knowledge that the soul receive there of God and of His love. Thanks to this knowledge, the presentiment of what will bring us the clear vision of God in glory increases in intensity."[16]

A gas filled balloon

Outwardly there is no difference between people who are affected with this spiritual sickness and those who are not. Interiorly, it is the difference between a standard air filled party balloon and a hydrogen filled balloon, both balloons look alike. However, when you let go an air filled balloon it will immediately fall to the ground. The opposite is the case when you release a gas filled balloon; it instantly levitates skyward. Similarly, the soul filled with the Holy Spirit is in a constant state of inward straining heavenward. According to John of the cross the reason for this painful inner tension is because the soul is constrained by the tread of life itself and cannot fly to God. That in essence is the torment that dominates the mystical way, namely the extreme longing to be with God in Paradise.

---

[16] Woman Mystics (Louis Bouyer) page 189 - Ignatius Press San Francisco

When Jesus was preaching the Good News He told the people *"The Kingdom of God is near! Turn away from your sins and believe the Good News"* (Mark 1:14-15) It is only in conversion (turning away from sin) that we are set free to respond to God's love. Only then do we grasp the meaning of what Jesus said, *"Set your hearts on his Kingdom first, and on God's saving justice and all these other things will be given you as well".*(Matthew 6: 33). Later on Jesus is more explicit *"Anyone who loves me will keep my word, and my Father will love him, and we shall come to him and make a home in him."* [17] It is not a case of the Blessed Trinity transmigrating to new accommodation, it is the individual elevated to a higher state of God consciousness. One is reminded of the discovery of Saint Augustine of Hippo of the presence of God within him.

His Kingdom is truly within

No human being could mimic this phenomenon by any process of transcendental meditation or esoteric practises. One could sit mediating in the lotus position all day and night and all one will get is cramps, back pain and a vacuous mental state. *"**We** shall come to him and make **Our** home in him."* All human beings have a capacity for God, nevertheless, the initiative comes from

---

[17] John 14:23

God and not from man. It is God who tears from top to bottom the curtain of inner consciousness to reveal His presence. It is He Who put in the plumbing system and it is He Who produced the water (Holy Spirit) to flow through it, if you will. Christians experience the validation of Sacred Scripture when they experience in some measure the presence of God within them. As fire is also representative of the Holy Spirit one is immediately reminded of the biblical image of Moses looking in wonder at the non-consuming burning bush. If we could see the Holy Spirit within us we too would gaze in wonder.

One advances into this higher state only by the direct action of the Holy Spirit

When I mention contemplation I am referring to the state of infused or supernatural contemplation that John of the Cross wrote about for his fellow religious, a state superior to mediation. St. John of the Cross wrote for those already advanced in prayer living consecrated contemplative lives behind the cloister. However, it would be utterly wrong to assume that God restricts this grace to religious only. It goes without saying we cannot win this grace for ourselves. No matter how holy and knowledgeable spiritual directors may be, they are powerless to open the door to supernatural contemplation. One can only advance into infused contemplation by the direct action of the Holy Spirit.

This is much more likely to happen to individuals who practice 'True devotion to Mary. The reason for this is that although the conferring of this grace is the prerogative of the Holy Spirit, nevertheless, it is a wonderful thing to realise that whenever Our Lady knocks on the door of contemplation on our behalf, that door will always open! It stands to reason if there were more devotees of Mary there would be more Christian mystics.

Mary is our mother

At a time of her choosing Mary will lead those who are intimate with her through the narrow door of contemplation. Christians ought to take on board what Mr Duff makes very clear, namely, that **"Mary is our mother. But she can nourish the soul only in the measure that it depends on her and works in union with her."**[18] Another important consideration is that Our Lady does not abandon her spiritual children halfway. She will only cut the umbilical cord when we are in the vestibule of heaven. According to St Augustine, in Mary souls are born into Paradise by the power of the Holy Spirit. The logic is that as Mary gave birth to Jesus, the head of His Mystical Body, she consequently gives birth to all the members of His Mystical Body, the Church.

---

[18] The De Montfort Way by Frank Duff page 5

Having apprehended the object of one's interior gaze, the individual now longs with supernatural desire to go to God. Consequently, as we have already pointed out there is no cure for the phenomenon of the sickness of love; death itself is the only cure. St. Therese reflects this attitude of soul in one of her poems, "Life of an instant your burden is so heavy to me!"[19] Christ wounded by sin, responds in like manner and wounds with Love. For the Christian mystic the pendulum swings between two extremes, inner joy and dire longing, what may be called 'the agony and ecstasy' of mystical life. Cut deep into the psyche of the contemplative and you will discover the turbulent waters of the 'torment of the mystical way', namely, the very real thirst that cannot be quenched in this life. The Catechism affirms this reality, "Thirst for God is quenched by the waters of eternal life." John 4:14 (CCC 2557) It is one of the antimonies of spiritual life, the more we drink of the Spirit, the more we thirst for God.

Your life must be controlled by love

Examine the life of the Saints and you will discover that all of them had an innate passion to save souls from eternal separation from God. St Therese of the Child Jesus in her 'Act of Oblation as victim of God's Merciful

---

[19] 'Living on Love'

Love' gives us her ulterior motive for her passion to save souls, **"I wish to labour for thy Love alone** – with the sole aim of pleasing Thee, of consoling Thy Sacred Heart, and of saving souls who will love Thee throughout eternity." For the Little Flower, love of Jesus Christ was the motive of all her actions. She knew that God Who is Merciful Love cannot but thirst to give of Himself. Likewise individuals caught up in the Trinitarian flames of love instinctively feel the need to give of themselves to others; to live in love for Love. That's what St Paul indicates when he wrote to the Ephesians *"Since you are God's dear children, you must try to be like him. Your life must be controlled by love."* [20] St Peter echoes Paul's exhortation *"From now on, then, you must live the rest of your earthly lives controlled by God's will and not your own."* (Peter 1:4-2)

Draw me

The simple truth is individuals that have surrendered to the will of God allow God to draw them. They may say: *"Draw me: we will run after Thee to the odour of Thy ointments."* I shall let the great Mystical Doctor St Therese of the Child Jesus explain those words of the Canticles[21]: Addressing Jesus she says: "O my Jesus, there is no need to say. In drawing me, draw also the

---

[20] Ephesians 5:1-2 see also Ephesians 5 for the fruits of the Holy Spirit.
[21] Canticle of Canticles 1:3 or Song of Songs in updated NRSV Bibles.

souls that I love: these words, *"Draw me"*, suffice. When a soul has let herself be taken captive by the inebriating odour of Thy perfumes she cannot run alone; as a natural consequence of her attraction towards Thee, the souls of all those she loves are drawn in her train. Just as a torrent carries into the depths of the sea all that it meets on its way, so, my Jesus does the soul who plunges into the shoreless ocean of Thy Love bring with it all its treasures."[22]

The greatest love we can show our neighbour is to give him Christ his Saviour

Church history has conclusively demonstrated that souls possessed by the Holy Spirit become imbued with a connatural propensity to externalise that love by guiding others into the fellowship of Jesus Christ because "The greatest love we can show our neighbour is to give him Christ his Saviour."[23] The reality is "A soul that is burning with love cannot remain inactive"[24] This indicates no matter what way you look at it, the apostolate flows out from the bedrock of love for God. Wherever God is not loved, there will be no consideration for the salvation of souls. On the other hand, if there is genuine solicitude for the salvation of others, you will discover authentic Christian mysticism. The genius of Frank Duff was to release that untapped

---

[22] The Story of a Soul, chapter XI – A Canticle of Love
[23] BY THE WORKING OF THE HOLY SPIRIT by Fr. John Ahern ch 7 page 76
[24] St Therese of the Child Jesus

wellspring of authentic love for God by harnessing ordinary men and women to the operations of the Holy Spirit, in other words, he has universalized the apostolate of the Catholic Church at a critical era of the 20th Century. In doing so he effectively demystifies mysticism by reducing it to its basic constituents namely, love of God and neighbour. He did not depend unduly on sensate charismatic frills yet he lived in union with Mary at the highest level of mystical life.

Enter Saint Louis Marie DeMontfort

No Saint has played a greater part in the development of the Legion than this French missionary. He is really the tutor of the Legion. - Very Rev. Francis J Canon Ripley

Frank Duff's practical spiritual booklet, "Can we be Saints?" exposed his well-developed spirituality and eschatological orientation; best expressed by his striving to be a Saint. The book was written sometime before the Legion of Mary came into existence in 1921. However, like countless devote Catholics of that era he lacked the essential knowledge that gave rise to a more comprehensive understanding of the Virgin Mary's role in the economy of salvation. One does not imply that Frank Duff was ever lacklustre in his devotion to Mary; there is no question of that. Fortunately he was open to the Holy Spirit, therefore the stage was providentially set; enter Blessed Louis Marie Grignion DeMontfort as he was known then, with his theological masterpiece on Our Lady know today as 'True Devotion to the Blessed Virgin Mary'.

A book of high authority and unction

To this moment in time DeMontfort's precious writings, particularly his Marian treatise issue forth a mysterious power that has influenced countless Christians to enter into a formal act of consecration to the Mother of God. Pope St. Leo XIII granted a plenary indulgence to those who make St. Louis Marie De Montfort's act of consecration to the Blessed Virgin. When the Pope was dying he renewed his act of consecration to Our Lady and invoked the aid of DeMontfort whom he had beatified in 1888.[1] Rev Fr. Francis J Ripley, a personal friend and confidant of Frank Duff for many years has put on record, "No Saint has played a greater part in the development of the Legion than this French missionary. He is really the tutor of the Legion. The Handbook is full of his spirit. The prayers re-echo his very words."[2] St Louis Marie was a Catholic priest whose lifespan was 43years (1673 – 1716). During his extraordinary life he drank deeply from the 'inner cellar' of mystical union with the Blessed Virgin and took pen to paper and wrote his now famous treatise, of which Pope Benedict XV described as, "A book of high authority and unction." Everywhere he went he preached Christ crucified and stressed the huge importance of the daily recitation of the Rosary. His book 'The Secret of the Rosary' is also a spiritual classic along with his lesser- known work, "The Love of Eternal Wisdom."

---

[1] Preliminary notes to True Devotion to Mary – Tan books - 1985
'Talks to Legionaries' by Rev Francis J. Ripley (1963) Article 25

His biographers tell us everywhere Fr. Louis Marie De Montfort went in his native country he prayed aloud and sang the praises of God. "He is the poorest of the poor living most of his life on what divine Providence gave to him in the ways of alms." His existential poverty was an outward manifestation of his interior state of poverty. Those who knew Frank Duff personally would have observed this similar virtue in him. De Montfort understood that "True greatness is to be found in the soul, not in a name,"[3] he simply preferred everyone to address him as 'DeMontfort' meaning from Montfort the place of his birth. Louis was his baptismal name and he acquired the name Marie (Mary) when he made his Confirmation. Like St John Bosco he was endowed with great physical strength and it may come as a shock to some but he wasn't afraid to use his fists to put manners on some of the miscreants who tried to upstage him while he was preaching.

Everyone who studies the True Devotion will fall beneath its spell

His 'True Devotion to Mary' may have little appeal to those not earnestly seeking to advance in grace. De Montfort maintained that without a tender love for Mary, souls are in danger of losing all their spiritual treasures. Even those 'Giant Cedars of Lebanon', that is to say,

---

[3] St Therese of the Child Jesus (Story of a Soul – chapter 6)

those advanced in holiness are in danger of crashing down and losing everything. For that reason DeMontfort said, "God wishes that His holy Mother should be at present more known and loved, more honoured than she has ever been." Therefore he urged every baptised person to go down on their knees and pray earnestly to the Holy Spirit so as to be "cast in her as in a perfect mould of Jesus Christ." The Servant of God, Frank Duff said regarding his writing, "It is certain that everyone who studies the True Devotion will fall beneath its spell, for the book has everything."[4]

The square peg of Frank's airtight Catholicism

It's interesting to note that Mr Duff's first reading of the Marian Treatise seems to have unsettled him a little. One has to bear in mind that he was in the afterglow of the success of his inspiring booklet, "Can we be saints?" in which he spoke about devotion to Mary in glowing terms. His little book was no mean achievement for a layperson without any formal theological training. Intelligent, a top civil servant and with a practical and methodical frame of mind, he considered De Montfort's claims about Our Lady to be far-fetched. His Marian Theology didn't quite fit into the square peg of Frank's airtight Catholicism at that particular time. If this French mystic is correct, that would imply that his own Marian perspective was somewhat flawed. Indeed, one may be

---

[4] The De Montfort Way by Frank Duff page 10.

tempted to consider that his reading of the treatise unsweetened the hubris that accompanies a successful publication.

The most direct route to transformation in Jesus Christ

Up until Vatican II it was necessary for a Catholic writer to have their work theologically (imprimatur) approved if they wished to have it published. Ecclesiastical Authority stamped its seal of approval on Frank's booklet; he had not compromised truth in any way. Yet, this little known Frenchman who bore the title 'Blessed' preached slavery to Mary, a devotion that surpassed the commonly held Catholic view of the day. De Montfort boldly advocated handing over ones entire life to Our Lady as the most direct route to transformation in Jesus Christ. Like other great personages Frank's early readings of 'True Devotion to Mary,' meant that the veracity of De Montfort's claims eluded him. Even to this day, there are well informed Catholics who have difficulty in accepting the 'True Devotion' and even having taking up the practise don't quite realise the extraordinary importance of consecration to the Immaculate Heart of Mary.

I had not the degree of knowledge which would be necessary to absorb the True Devotion

At the time Frank was active in the Vincent De Paul Society and had become a daily Mass goer, yet he was ill-equipped to appreciate the theological brilliance of this missionary Priest. Frank was like a person who looked at the clock but lacked the ability to tell the time. Nevertheless, his preliminary contact with this powerful book did secretly release the spores of divine unction within him to the extent it exposed his lack of Marian Theology and left a nagging question ringing in his consciousness. Was there more to devotion to Our Lady other than what he was brought up to believe? Although, like many Irish Catholics of his day Frank Duff had a strong devotion to Our Lady, he was obliged to make a candid confession, "In my case I had not the degree of knowledge which would be necessary to absorb the True Devotion. Indeed, it appeared to me to border on the absurd." However, with his rational mind stirred he earnestly sought to correctly place the decimal point in regards Our Lady's true status within the framework of the divine economy. He set about getting to "know her sublime dignity, her grand agency in the mystery of redemption, her graces, her virtues, her merits, her agency in the salvation of every one of us."[5]

Enter Father Januarius De Concilio

Frank spent a few days with his friend, Joe Gabbett, at the Cistercian Abbey of Mt Mellery situated in the beautiful hilly countryside of County Waterford. On his

---

[5] The Knowledge of Mary (1878) Fr. Januarius De Concilio - Introduction - page 30.

arrival at the Monastery he asked for the loan of a book that would help him understand the theology of the Blessed Virgin Mary. He is handed a copy of Father De Concilio's theological work 'The Knowledge of Mary.' Frank Duff was so taken with this book that he buzzed with excitement and enthusiastically began to copy page after page. He tells us that this book give him the key to understanding DeMontfort's claims about Mary. Fr. DeConcilio taught him that "Mary is the epitome, the recapitulation of Catholic theology."[6] Sometime after that Frank once again takes up the enigmatic treatise and with a more informed mindset reads through it again. He did this more than once. In the process he scratches beneath the surface, if you will, and discovers the pure gold of DeMontfort's prophetic masterpiece. A bolt of pure white illumination arched across his intellect revealing the primary colours of truth concerning Our Lady's role in the plan of salvation and her unique mission.

A way to worship God that will please him, with reverence and awe

Frank's reading of the works of DeConcilio and DeMontfort, which he referred to as interdependent halves, gave him much more than mere theological insights. He absorbed something of their spirit. It was a veritable transmission of Charismata, if you will. One can only marvel at the spiritual power that was unleashed

---

[6] Ibid

upon him. Now he could appreciate what De Montfort was advocating, namely, *a way to worship God that will please him, with reverence and awe.*[7] A type of chemical reaction occurs illuminating him as to the vast horizon of holiness through Mary with all its multitudinous implications. In the blink of an eye his understanding of Catholicism was greatly embellished. Frank now understood that a total dependence on Mary strengthens our relationship with the Holy Spirit. Providentially this priestly tag team handed the future founder of the Legion of Mary the Archimedean lever that would shift the gigantic stone that for centuries blocked the way for the masses of lay people to engage comprehensively in the Church's apostolic mission. Effectively Frank Duff had woken the sleeping giant within the Mystical Body of Christ. He wrote, "DeMontfort attaches large promises to the worthy practise of the Devotion. It would be nothing less than a supreme tragedy if he were to be imagined as exaggerating, because he does not exaggerate in the slightest way. The soul that Mary is enabled to really mother grows beneath her touch." [8] From this point onwards Frank saw Our Lady as the Virgo Potens (Virgin most powerful) dressed in the 'Gold of Opher', that is to say, clothed in the splendour of the power of God. The fact that "Everything connected with the children of God is placed under her influence... She

---

[7] Hebrews 13:28
[8] True Devotion to Mary – St Paul's Publications – Foreword by Frank Duff

administers the divine life to them to grow up in Christ"[9]had a monumental impact on him.

Everything connected with the children of God is placed under her influence

In each generation it seems a sense of the Infinite becomes under attack from all quarters, particularly so in this sophisticated generation. DeMontfort saw that True devotion to Mary is the antidote to the malaria of secularism. Like flashing lightning striking a night seascape the Son of God touched down on humanity at the Incarnation and illuminated the glorious horizon where the Infinite merges with the finite. Mary's 'fiat' made that possible. Mary became the 'flux capacitor' if you will, that channels the divine life upon humanity. She is truly the cause of our joy securing for us the formula for infinite happiness *"Do whatever he tells you."* (Luke 2:5) In Mary water will change into wine and impossibilities become realities.

Mary's work and the work of the Holy Spirit as one inseparable movement

It was only a matter of time until the Holy Spirit would give Frank Duff the charism of Our Lady herself by allowing him to enter into that sacred noosphere that exists between Himself and Our Lady. His heart was twinned with the Immaculate Heart of Mary. What

---

[9] True Devotion to Mary by DeMontfort - Introduction

DeMontfort maintained became a reality in him "The soul of Mary will be communicated to you to glorify the Lord. Her Spirit will take the place of yours to rejoice in God, her Saviour'. (TD 217) His spirit leaped for joy within him and the Holy Spirit raised him far above the level of mere respect and gratitude to a new level of consciousness. He now realised that concentrated within Mary is the whole salvific economy[10]. As two rivers merged into one, creating one fast moving torrent, he understood, "Mary's work' and the work of the Holy Spirit are one inseparable movement. However, here we ought to make a distinction; it is not Mary's power at work, rather it is the incomprehensible power of the Holy Spirit issuing through her. All the gifts, virtues and graces of the Holy Ghost are distributed by Mary, to who she wishes, when she wishes, the way she wishes and as much as she wishes."[11] Frank Duff's undertaking of the metaphysics of 'true devotion' meant that he handed his whole life to Mary for the glory of God and the salvation of souls, even the cash crop of his own merits. With great energy he willingly embraced DeMontfort's True Devotion. In response, Mary gave to him *the key that opens all the hidden treasures of God's wisdom and knowledge.* (Col 2:3). In Duff's writings particularly the handbook of the Legion of Mary you will discover the golden nuggets of this wisdom and knowledge.

---

[10] Redemptoris Mater by Pope John Paul II Number 36
[11] T. D. 141 –page 90 – St. Bernard, Inter opera. Meditation on the knowledge of our human condition

There is no grace which Mary cannot dispose of as her own

St Maximilian Kolbe a renowned exponent of DeMontfort's True Devotion pointed out, "The union between the Immaculata and the Holy Spirit is so inexpressible, yet so perfect that the Holy Spirit acts only by the Immaculata, His Spouse. This is why she is the Mediatrix of all Graces given by the Holy Spirit." He goes on to explain…. "All grace is a gift from God the Father, through the Son and by means of the Holy Spirit. It follows that there is no grace which Mary cannot dispose of as her own and which is not given to her for this purpose."[12]

Mary's motherhood is really an infinite thing because God has made it part of His own parenthood

Under the impulse of the Holy Spirit Frank Duff begins to plant the seeds of True Devotion in the field of the 'Royal Priesthood' of the Laity, incorporating it into the Legion system. In a practical way he opened the way for every layperson to give everything to Jesus through Mary: our personality with all its thoughts and emotions, our memory, will and understanding. One of the supreme benefits of this act of consecration to Mary is that it also leads the individual into a deeper relationship with Our Heavenly Father. Frank experienced this dynamic for himself. He wrote, "We plunge ourselves into Mary's

---

'Pray Pray Pray' by Rev. Dr. Gerard McGinnity page 174

motherhood and Mary's motherhood is really an infinite thing because God has made it part of His own parenthood." [13]   At this stage it seems appropriate to apply the words of Wisdom (7:26) to Our Lady, *"She is a reflection of eternal light, a spotless mirror of God's action and an image of his goodness."*

St Louis Marie de Montfort, pray for us

In the handbook there is an acknowledgement to De Montfort:
"In view of the other decisions as to the inadmissibility of particular and local patrons, the inclusion of the name of Blessed Grignion de Montfort would at first sight appear to be debatable ground. It can, however, be safely asserted that no saint has played a greater part in the development of the Legion than he. The handbook is full of his spirit. The prayers re-echo his very words. He is really the tutor of the Legion: thus invocation is due to him by the Legion almost as a matter of moral obligation." (Decision of the Legion placing the name of Blessed Grignion de Montfort in the list of invocations) 'St. Louis Marie de Montfort, pray for us'. He was canonised on 20 July, 1947, his feast-day is celebrated on the 28th April."

---

[13] Woman of Genesis by Frank Duff – article 'Have the mind of Mary'

The Legion of Mary precipitated his status of 'Blessed' to that of Sainthood

Ever since its discovery in 1842[14] the 'True devotion' has had an incontrovertibly effect upon the Catholic Church. Before his book was sanctioned by the magisterium it had undergone a test of fire. It was not until 12th May 1853[15] that the decree was pronounced at Rome declaring his book to be exempt from all error which could be a bar to his canonization. Since then his celebrated treatise on Our Lady has had phenomenal success. One may open the official manual of the Legion on almost any page and inhale not only the spirit of its founder but that of St. Louis Marie De Montfort. The Legion reaches out with the maternal arms of Mary to embrace the whole world for Christ, for that reason the Legion of Mary is in essence nothing more than the Spiritual Motherhood of Our Lady in action. It is largely due to the Legion that St. Louis- Marie Grignion is now a household name. Indeed, many have expressed the view that the birth of the Legion of Mary precipitated his status of 'Blessed' to that of Sainthood. It is impossible to predict when, if ever, Christianity will reach an apogee in Marian devotion. However, it cannot be denied that DeMontfort has elevated devotion to Our Lady to a whole new dimension and given humanity a firewall against the cultural deluge of secularism.

---

[14] France - St. Laurent sur Sevre
[15] 'True Devotion to Mary' translation by Father Faber's Preface - Tan books and Publishers, INC. Rockford, Illinois – 1985 edition

One will also find in the Legion handbook a portion of the tribute that Cardinal Federigo Tedeschini gave at the unveiling of the statue of St. Louis-Marie de Montfort in Saint Peter's, 8 December 1948. It gives us a clearer understanding of the man himself:

"Not only a founder, but missionary as well! And more than missionary; for we see yet another aspect: He is doctor and theologian, who has given us a Mariology such as no one before him had conceived. So deeply has he explored the roots of Marian devotion, so widely has he extended its horizons, that he has become without question the announcer of all the modern manifestations of Mary – from Lourdes to Fatima, from the definition of the Immaculate Conception to the Legion of Mary. He has constituted himself the herald of the coming of the reign of God through Mary, and the precursor of that longed-for salvation which in the fullness of time the Virgin Mother of God will bring to the world by her Immaculate Heart."

Devotion to Mary leads one to be entirely open to the action of the Holy Spirit

DeMontfort discovered a secret of grace, a garden enclosed within a garden, if you will. *"My sister, My spouse, is a garden enclosed, a garden enclosed, a fountain sealed up."* (Cant 4:12) "Mary is shut, Mary is sealed. The miserable children of Adam and Eve, driven from the earthly paradise, cannot enter into one except by a particular grace of the Holy Spirit, which they must merit." (TD 263) Since he has told us his secret, it is no longer a secret. In 1858 Our Lady at Lourdes confirmed this by the mysterious event of the uncovering of the hidden fountain, when at Mary's instructions, little Bernadette uncovered the hidden spring. Thus, it may be said that Mary herself cut the ribbon to the grand opening of the 'New Age of Mary' in the life of the Church. O wonderful paradox! One can never repeat too often that true devotion to Mary leads one to be entirely open to the action of the Living Water – the Holy Spirit. Our Lady always invites the whole of humanity to drink from this inexhaustible spring of grace. Oh, but here there is a real danger of missing the point or to put it another way of letting the 'Secret of Mary' trickle through our fingers. It is the Holy Spirit that gives to each person with the right disposition the key to the secret garden where one may drink from the fountain of spiritual intimacy with the Mother of Jesus for the benefit of their souls. It was the Holy Spirit who initiated Frank Duff into a profound intimate relationship with Our Lady. "Oh, how happy is the man who has given everything to Mary, and has entrusted himself to Mary, and lost himself in her, in everything and for everything!" exclaimed DeMontfort. (TD 179)

Throughout his priestly ministry DeMontfort complained "Jesus is not known as He ought." He interprets the reason for this as a lack of true devotion to Our Lady. He goes on to explain: "When the Holy Spirit, her Spouse, has found Mary in a soul, he flies there. He enters there in His fullness. He communicates Himself to that soul abundantly, and to the full extent to which it makes room for His Spouse. Nay, one of the greatest reasons why the Holy Spirit does not now do startling wonders in our souls is because He does not find there a sufficiently great union with His faithful and inseparable spouse. I say "inseparable" spouse, because since that Substantial Love of the Father and the Son has espoused Mary, in order to produce Jesus Christ, the Head of the elect, and Jesus Christ in the elect, He has never repudiated her, because she has always been fruitful and faithful."(TD 36)

Totus tuus

Saint John Paul II referred to De Montfort as a 'Theologian of class'. He recalls: "I often remember a 'little book' with the blue cover dirty with soda…When I used to work by the Solvay, I always brought that book with me, together with a piece of bread for the afternoon and night - shifts. During the morning shift it was difficult to read, while during the afternoon I could read that little book. Its title was "True Devotion to Mary". I used to read it many times from beginning to the last page and thanks to that book I discovered the real devotion to Mary. Before reading that book, I thought that praying to the Holy Virgin meant to hide the love for Jesus Christ. While reading 'True Devotion to Mary', I finally discovered the contrary, that is, that our interior relationship with the Mother of God is but the consequence of our tie with the mystery of God." He went on to say "This 'perfect devotion' is indispensable to anyone who means to give himself without reserve to Christ and to the work of redemption. – "It is from Montfort that I have taken my motto: 'Totus tuus' ("All yours.")

He who shall find Mary shall find life

St Louis Marie's priestly life became a quest to 'spill the beans' on what he called the 'Secret of Mary'. He taught that "He who shall find Mary shall find life, that is, Jesus Christ, who is the Way, the Truth and the Life"[16] He travelled all over Brittany preaching Christ Crucified and true devotion to Mary. Bursting to tell the whole world of his discoveries, he may be compared to Marco Polo just back from a mysterious and wondrous land. He appears to be hyperventilating with joy; aglow with allegorical imagery in his eagerness to share what he experienced in the mystical Utopia or 'secret garden'[17]

---

[16] Reference to the Gospel of John 14:6
[17] True devotion to Mary 263 – (Cant 4:12)

of the Blessed Virgin Mary: "We must first know that our Blessed Lady is the true terrestrial paradise of the New Adam, and that the ancient paradise was but a figure of her. There are, then, in this earthly paradise, riches, beauties, rarities and inexplicable sweetness's, which Jesus Christ, the New Adam, has left there: it was in this paradise that He took his complacence for nine months, worked His wonders and displayed His riches with the magnificence of a God. This most holy place is composed only of a virginal and immaculate earth, of which the New Adam was formed, and on which He was nourished, without any spot or stain, by means of the work of the Holy Spirit, who dwelt there. It is in this earthly paradise that there is the true tree of life, which has borne Jesus Christ, the Fruit of Life, and the tree of the knowledge of good and evil, which has given light unto the world. There are in this divine place trees planted by the hand of God and watered by His divine unction, which have born and bear fruits daily of a divine taste. There are flowerbeds adorned with beautiful and varied blossoms of virtues, diffusing odours which delight the very angels. There are meadows green with hope, impregnable towers of strength, and the most charming houses of confidence." ..."It is only the Holy Spirit who can make us know the hidden truth of these figures of material things. There is in this place an air of perfect purity; a fair sun, without shadow of Divinity; a fair day, without night, of the Sacred Humanity; a continual burning furnace of love, where all the iron that

is cast into it is changed, by excessive heat, into Gold."
(True Devotion 261)

The salvation of the world began through Mary and through her it must be accomplished

Frank Duff wrote in the Legion handbook: "The legionary seeking the Holy Spirit through Mary will receive abundantly of His gifts, and among these gifts will be a truly enlightened love of Mary herself." Conversely by means of consecration to the Immaculate Heart of Mary we will experience Our Lady's maternal touch in our own lives and her unique Charism will lead us to intimacy with her Son and the Holy Spirit. In the company of Our Lady the Holy Spirit seems quite content to communicate grace through Mary, that is to say, through the modality of Mary's spiritual motherhood of souls. He first spoke definitively in Mary, in that He made the 'Word' flesh in her. In so doing, He established his modus operandi. Hence St. Louis Marie de Montfort pointed out, "The salvation of the world began through Mary and through her it must be accomplished." (TD 49) He goes on to say, "If devotion to Our Lady removed us from Jesus Christ, we should have to reject it as an illusion of the devil; but so far from being the case, true devotion to Our Lady is, on the contrary, necessary for us – as a means of finding Jesus perfectly, of loving Him tenderly, of serving Him faithfully."(TD 62) The Servant of God is of the same conviction, "Love of Mary is a quality which must proceed from every Christian. The fact of this matter is that love of Mary is obligatory on every member of the Mystical Body, just as Faith is obligatory on every member. Faith in Jesus Christ and love of Mary are the basic requirements – the foundation stones of Christianity, without which salvation is a doubtful proposition."[18] These statements unequivocally lay the axe to the false notion that devotion to Mary is a kind of optional extra, something tagged on to Christian devotional practise.

Mighty legion of brave and valiant solders

In these turbulent times the Church recognises Saint Louis Marie De Montfort as a voice crying in the wildernesses to make straight a highway for the second coming of the Lord Jesus Christ[19] - that highway is the Blessed Virgin Mary. He prophetically stated: "In these latter times Mary must shine forth more than ever in mercy, power and grace; in mercy, to bring back and welcome lovingly the poor sinners and wanderers who are to be converted and return to the Catholic Church; in power, to combat the enemies of God who will rise up menacingly to seduce and crush by promises and threats all those who oppose them; finally, she must shine forth in grace to inspire and support the valiant soldiers and

---

[18] Mary Shall Reign by Frank Duff – article 'Thinking in Christ'.
[19] Luke 3:4

loyal servants of Jesus Christ who are fighting for his cause." (TD 50: 6)

The Legion of Mary is the fulfilment of DeMontfort's prophetic intuition

His mantra or cry, 'To Jesus, through Mary' will not cease to echo in the corridors of the Catholic Church until the close of time. In that context the Legion of Mary echoes that same cry in its apostolic mission. I, like many others, am warming to the opinion that the Legion of Mary is the fulfilment of DeMontfort's prophetic intuition. "It even gives me encouragement to hope for a great success at the prospect of a mighty legion of brave and valiant soldiers of Jesus and Mary, both men and women, who will fight the devil, the world, and corrupt nature in the perilous times that are sure to come." (TD 114) If this is not so, in what secret outpost is that other 'mighty legion of brave and valiant solders' hiding and what will it take to draw them out to high enterprise for Christ the King?

Enter Saint Therese
of the Child Jesus   Chapter 4

I beg you to cast your divine glance upon a great number of little souls. I beg you to choose a legion of little Victims worthy of your love. - St Therese of the Child Jesus

If one compares the life of Francis Duff of Dublin with that of Francis of Assisi one is immediately struck with the outward display of the miraculous in the life of the Stigmatic. By contrast there appears to be little of the outward signs of the miraculous in the life of Frank Duff. Being so ordinary, one may easily miss the extraordinary, as indeed was the case in the life of St. Therese of Lisieux. Who in the Carmelite convent at the time could ever have imagined that this young girl would be crowned Saint and Doctor of the Church, in less than a hundred years? Pope Pius X went on to say that she was "the greatest Saint in modern times" The Church celebrates her feastday on the 1st October.

Her image suddenly came alive

By way of making this chapter more interesting and less abstract, I will share my own little encounter with this remarkable Saint. One day, in my early teens, I made a visit to the Blessed Sacrament in a Church I had not visited before. I said my few prayers and headed out through the side porch. On my way I noticed a picture of an unfamiliar Saint hanging on the wall. As I was looking at the picture, her image suddenly came alive and this lovely young lady smiled at me, or more correct to say, she laughed at me in the way a parent would laugh at a child that did something silly. This phenomenon only lasted 10 seconds or so. I thought no more about it until, sometime later, Fr. Mark C.P. my Novice Master handed me a book to read, it was called 'The Autobiography of a Saint' another name for 'The Story of a Soul'. When I opened the cover my heart skipped a beat; to my utter surprise there was the same image of Therese who introduced herself to me less than 18 months earlier. To this day I remember the happiness I had in reading that wonderful book. Fr. Mark said I was a slow reader but the truth is I was so reluctant to hand it back; I kept on re-reading it.

I demand another mother to assist me

Not surprising, you will notice her words running like a golden thread though the chapters of my book. I confess, since my youth Therese has been like a big sister to me. I remember many years ago in a holy stupor making my way back to work after attending the 12:00 lunchtime Mass, when I experienced Jesus telling me plainly that I was, in the spiritual order the weakest of souls and that He compared me to a special needs child. I immediately shot back at Him, 'If that's the case, I should be given another mother to assist me.' His reply was instant, "I already have!" Taken back a little, I replied, 'who is she?' Jesus answered, "Therese of the Child Jesus!" I realised that this interior conversation was no figment of a fertile imagination, as it explained the extraordinary intervention of the Little Flower ever since she made herself known to me all those years ago. The words of Jesus stirred up the beautiful imagery I had when I left the Passionist Monastery at Minsteracres, Co Durham after a blissful two year stay with them, between the ages of 16/18 years. In a sort of dream I saw a little duckling flanked by two large white swans heading out of the harbour towards the open sea. I instantly understood the duckling to be me and the swans to be Our Lady and St Therese; my two spiritual mothers! In the choppy waters of life they have made their presence felt in many wonderful ways. I realised it was the Holy Spirit who introduced me to this great Saint for the benefit of my soul. I urge everyone to read her 'The Story of a Soul' and reap the benefits. After that digression I will crack on with what I have to say about St Therese regarding the founder of the Legion of Mary.

Trapped by Providence in the crossbeams of two great French luminaries

One does not deny that during his life Frank Duff came under the influence of many great personages, such as writers G.K. Chesterton and Cardinal John Henry Newman. However in his twenties it cannot be denied he was trapped by Providence in the crossbeams of two great French luminaries, namely, St Therese of the Child Jesus and St Louis Marie De Montfort. Their influence on him was substantial. At the turn of the 20th century, prior to his encounter with DeMontfort's Treatise 'True Devotion to Mary' there was another far more readable book that took the Catholic world by storm. I am of course referring to the Autobiography of St Therese of Lisieux, universally known today as 'The Story of a Soul'; at the time it was 'all the go'. Sister Therese of the Child Jesus entitled her memoirs: 'The Story of the springtime of a Little White Flower.' It could well have been titled, 'Christian Mysticism for Dummies'. I am inclined to believe Divine Providence had ordained that 'The Story of a Soul' should fall into the hands of a young Frank Duff prior to his encounter with St Louis Marie De Montfort. I am correct to assume that Therese Martin got to Frank Duff first and taught him her Little Way of Spiritual childhood the cornerstone on which True Devotion to Mary rests; on the truth that God is our Father and Mary is our mother and we are their children.

Little Flower

At the time Therese Martin was not even a 'Blessed'.[1] Prior to her canonisation in 1925 by Pope Pius X she

---

[1] Therese's beatification – 29th April, 1923

was universally known as the 'Little Flower.' Holy pictures of her appeared everywhere and the manufacturers of statues were kept busy. Writers of Catholic spirituality began to feed like locusts on her little book. It is no surprise that Frank mentioned her in his first publication. "Can we be saints?" In fact he seems to have laid his pen to rest in her honour by allowing her to have the final word. He wrote: "With the Little Flower – we will cry out in longing" "Jesus! Jesus! I would so wish to love you…love you as you never yet have been loved." These passionate sentiments expressed the core meaning of her short life[2] and revealed the interior disposition of Frank Duff. I think it fair to say it also revealed the sentiments of the Legion of Mary envoy to Africa, the Venerable Edel Quinn. As a matter of fact, Edel's friend Mary Walls is on record as saying "The Life and other writings of the Little Flower were great favourites. In fact, the book entitled L'Esprit de Sainte Therese became one of her most cherished possessions. She had it in French and evidently applied herself to living constantly according to its teaching."

After my death I shall let fall a shower of roses

This young Carmelite nun was so on fire with love for Jesus that she desired to come back to earth after death to make Jesus known and loved. "After my death I shall let fall a shower of roses." The sweet odour of these

---

[2] 1873 - 1897

'roses'(graces) and her theology of Spiritual Childhood (her 'Little Way') are inextricably interwoven into the fabric of the traditional life of the Catholic Church and hence into the apostolate of the Legion of Mary. Frank Duff included five references to St Therese in the handbook. One has to consider there can be no symbiotic relationship with Our Lady without the virtue of spiritual childhood. In fact, just as a flame has three essential elements namely, heat, light and colour, it may be said that the 'True Devotion' has three essential elements. They are intimacy with the Holy Spirit of Jesus and His Blessed Mother. Spiritual Childhood, and the Apostolate; they are interdependent and constitute the essential ingredients of mystical union with Mary.

'Little Daisy' stands resplendent among the majestic Roses

Therese Martin, her family name, is still to this day commonly known worldwide as the Little Flower. Her autobiography which she wrote under obedience has had an incalculable impact upon the Catholic Church for over the last hundred years or so. Like Frank Duff, Therese did not have a degree in Theology or Philosophy. In fact she had very little formal education and yet she excelled in what matters most in life, namely, holiness. In common with the Servant of God, Frank Duff, she loved God above every other human being and everything else in life; both in their own particular way were teachers of the science of Love.

Mother Church was quick to recognise her sanctity and her wisdom by conferring her Saint and later Doctor of the Church. This is extraordinary, as there were only two women Doctors of the Church before that, St. Catherine of Siena and St. Teresa of Avila. How is it that this 'little Daisy' stands resplendent among the majestic roses, that is to say, the great Saints and scholarly Doctors of the Church. The answer to that question is found on the lips of Our Saviour: *"Father, Lord of heaven and earth! I thank you because you have shown to the unlearned what you have hidden from the wise and learned.* (Luke 10:21) Fr. Marie Eugene of the Child Jesus a devotee of Therese recalls a conversation he had with a blood sister of St. Therese: "One day, in a conversation with Sister Genevieve – I often spoke with her and obviously tried to learn all her secrets – she said to me: "My Sister had no devotions" "Really she had no devotions?" "No, for example she did not share the popular devotion to the Sacred Heart." "Why not?" "Because they turned it into a devotion when it is really a form of worship, the worship of Love."[3]

Blessed are they who put their trust in God

Her approach to God was not to His Justice, rather to His Mercy; that's the core of her spirituality. There is no doubt that Therese warmed the Heart of Jesus and held

[3] UNDER THE TORRENT OF HIS LOVE BY French Carmelite - Fr. Marie-Eugene of the Child Jesus – page 39.

Him in the palm of her hand. She allowed Jesus to love her, warts and all. Unlike other saints Therese became a victim soul of God's Merciful Love, rather than to His Divine Justice. She did so in order to make up for those who did not love Jesus, claiming that there were no shortage of victim souls to His Justice. In her Story of a Soul she wrote "I know that God, He is a father, mother, who in order to be happy must have his child upon his knee, resting on his heart." Her childlike trust in God as a loving father precluded any unhealthy fear. *"Blessed are they who put their trust in God."* (Psalm 2) She added "There is no one who could frighten me, for I know too well what to believe concerning his mercy and love."

"A morning, golden and new'- a morning that would 'last for all time'

Recently I watched the film 'Babe', a heart-warming tale. What really charmed me about that film is the song farmer Hogget sang to the gravely ill piglet. When Babe exhibited signs of recovery and accepted nourishment through a baby's bottle, farmer Hogget burst into song. "If I had words to make a day for you, I would sing you a morning golden and true; I would make it last for all time ......" His rapturous joy is so great that song gives way to dance; he takes to the floor. The look of ecstasy on his face says it all - magical stuff! In a way that film prompts one to contemplate like St Therese the joy of the Eternal Father, when we, His adopted sons and daughters partake of the Divine nourishment of Holy Communion. Therese knew that God the Father had given to humankind something that no other earthly father could ever possibly give to his child, namely, "a morning, golden and new- a morning that would last for all time." In a **Word,** (Jesus Christ) God the Father made for us an eternal day. Catholic mystical life is about living in the perpetual now of the eternal today.

Why I love Thee, Mary

Frank Duff had a remarkable similarity to her virtues, especially her steely will, and her almost superhuman devotion to duty. Both individuals were remarkably intelligent. They each used their fastidious attention to duty as a modality of their expression of their love for God. In addition, they had a remarkable childlike trust in Our Lady. Like Frank Duff Therese burned with desire to make her loved. Love for Our Lady flowed naturally from her deep union with Jesus. With resounding logic she said, "Do not be afraid of loving the Blessed Virgin, too much: you can never love her enough. Jesus will be glad of your love for her because the Blessed Virgin is His Mother." Therese also exclaimed, "How I love the Blessed Virgin! Had I been a Priest, how I should have spoken of her." Her last poem, written in May 1897 **'Why I love Thee, Mary!'** highlights her childlike love for Mary. "…..Oh, let me tell thee face to face; And say to thee for evermore: I am Thy little child." There is nothing in her writings to suggest that she came in contact with DeMontfort's 'True Devotion'. Yet she understood the virtue of approaching the Blessed Trinity, through Mary. This is evident from her 'Act of Oblation as a Victim of Divine Love' when she offered herself as victim of God's Merciful Love, through Mary: "I offer Thee, O Blessed Trinity, my most dear Mother; it is to her I entrust my oblation, begging her to present it to Thee." Is this not an echo of DeMontfort's 'To Jesus through Mary' Marian theology?

Jesus wants to possess your heart completely

Frank Duff admitted that DeMontfort's Marian treatise had caused shock waves to register in his consciousness, which, as he put it "Turned his world upside-down." By contrast 'The Story of a Soul' had a more subtle impact on him, rather like a powerful Tsunami that passes silently almost unnoticed beneath a ship at sea. Frank experienced the unction that emanates from the pages of her autobiography, unction that comes from a soul transformed in God. Her writings are simple yet powerful. They appealed to Frank because they have less of the extraordinary and more of the ordinary; they were on the same wavelength. Therese's rock solid scripture based spirituality was a breath of fresh air to him and to the Church of the early 20th Century. Remarkably like St Louis Marie **"She longed for a legion of little souls who would make Love known, and this not only in monasteries but in cities, on the streets, wherever**

there are souls called by God to His divine intimacy."[4] Prophetically, Frank fulfilled her desire for a Legion of little souls.

The good God never asks the impossible

Therese stated, "When we cast our faults into the devouring fire of love with total childlike trust, how would they not be consumed so that nothing is left of them?" She passionately believed that if each person cast themselves into the burning flames of Merciful Love without any merits of their own that "every imperfection, like fire which transforms all things into itself…" they would be transformed into saints. Her conviction was shared by DeMontfort who also saw God as "a continual burning furnace of love, where all the iron that is cast into it is changed, by excessive heat, into Gold." (True Devotion 261) Frank Duff was in full agreement with the Little Flower when she said, "Jesus wants to possess your heart completely. He wants you to be a great saint. The good God never asks the impossible."

God has so much Love to give, and he can't do it; people present only their own merits, and these are so paltry

At times in the past the God of Mercy seemed to be eclipsed by a hash judgemental God. Frank Duff, like so many of his contemporaries at the turn of the century

---

[4] Under the Torrent of His Love – by Fr. Marie-Eugene of the Child Jesus – Introduction page 23

may have been exposed to the culture of excessive appeasement to divine Justice. Whereby, a person endeavoured to win favour with God, primarily by the strength of one's own virtues, merits and good works; to make oneself worthy of His love by high moral standing. Therese has things to say on the matter, "God has so much Love to give and he can't do it; people present only their own merits and these are so paltry." Some individuals even adopt a brutal attitude towards their own flesh. In the past religious books were heavily nuanced with admiration for those who imposed harsh almost superhuman penitential exercises upon themselves. How often do we read in the lives of the Saints; "He regularly scoured his body to blood for souls?"[5] That was largely the culture that prevailed during the lifetime of Therese; a culture that ran contrary to her 'Little Way of Spiritual Childhood'.

Bow and Sword

Holy Scripture tells us that redemption does not come by way of our merits. "*For it was not in my bow that I trusted, nor yet was I saved by my sword. All the day long our boast was in God and we praised your name without ceasing.*" (Psalm 43:7) The bow and sword, representative of our merits, are not what saves. St Augustine acknowledges this; "Before any good merits of mine, the Mercy of God came to me. Even though He

---

[5] Dominic the Preacher – by Barbara Cahill O.P.

found no good in me, He Himself made me good." Far from having an Angelic nature we are flawed human beings. Our efforts are necessary of course but holiness only comes to those who seek it with the sure knowledge that Jesus is our holiness. St. Therese acknowledged this reality when she said, "When the evening of life comes, I shall stand before Thee with empty hands, because I do not ask Thee my God, to take account of my works. All our good deeds are blemished in Thine eyes. I wish therefore to be robed with Thine own justice, and to receive from Thy love the everlasting gift of thyself."

The Legion of Mary is the way of Divine Mercy par-excellence

Her spark of genius lay in her discovery that Almighty God has a weakness, that is to say, she understood that God who is Love, has a need to love and be loved. This may explain the phenomena of countless weak and imperfect individuals identifying themselves with Therese. As future leader of the Legion of Mary, Frank's providential encounter with Therese Martin and her Little Way meant that the Legion did not get side tracked by an inordinate orientation towards the Justice of God by taking an ascetical approach. It must be stated the way of Divine Justice is not the Marian way. The Legion has always been the way of Divine Mercy par-excellence. It never points an accusing finger but seeks to lead everyone to the tribunal of Divine Mercy. It reflects the mindset of the Eternal Father whose gaze is ever fixed upon the horizon in hopeful anticipation of the return of his prodigal children[6]. It is true to say the Legion has no tolerance for those who overstep the boundaries of morality; it has only unconditional love for them. The Legion of Mary reflects the love of the heart of Mary for each of her children.

His delight is to be with the children of men

Therese understood Jesus does not demand brutal and bloody penitential acts on the body. Therese wanted us to believe that Jesus loves us exceedingly and that His *"delight is to be with the children of men.[7]"* Are not our bodies' temples of His Holy Spirit? Why vandalise the body as many saints have done in the past? What mother or father would allow their child to wear tight chains around its waist in their honour that might cut into the flesh and poison the bloodstream, or allow them to use stones for pillows? God does not require us to cut or damage our bodies. Of course, one is not saying that we should not do penance. However, we ought to do penance in a healthy and hygienic way that does not damage the body. Is God a blood thirsty Toltec or Aztec god who demands the perpetual bloodletting of his children? God desires only the sacrifice of praise and thanksgiving; our votive offering of love and the ringing out His goodness. (Grail-Psalm 49:14 + Psalm 50:16-17)

---

[6] Luke 15:11-12
[7] Proverbs 8:31

The Little Flower wanted everyone to become like a little child in the arms of their Heavenly Father. To allow Him to fulfil His need to love, by raising us up to the highest estate of mystical union with Him in the Blessed Trinity - to the ecstasy of love; to fly with Jesus, the Divine Eagle, infinitely higher than one's greatest expectations.

He takes into account our weakness, that he is perfectly aware of our fragile nature

St Therese wrote in chapter 9 of her story of a soul, "In order that Love may be fully satisfied it is necessary that It lower Itself, and that It lower Itself to nothingness and transform this nothingness in *fire*" In a moment of lovesick madness the Creator broke the Triune seal to pour out Love upon all humanity[8]. That seal was definitively broken when the lance pieced the Heart of Jesus Christ, font of Merciful Love. In the light of which, Therese wrote with interior certitude "To me God has granted His infinite Mercy, and through it I contemplate and adore the other divine perfections! All these perfections appear to be resplendent with love; even His Justice seems to me clothed in love. What a sweet joy it is to think that God is Just, i.e., that He takes into account our weakness, that he is perfectly aware of our fragile nature. What should I fear then? Ah! Must not the infinitely just God, who deigns to pardons the faults

---

[8] John 3:16

of the prodigal son with so much kindness, be just also towards me who 'am with Him always"? That's the language of a mystic whose own heart has been wounded by Love in order for her to become an apostle of Merciful Love to the whole world.

No other Throne, no other Crown, but Jesus Himself

During her teenage years St Therese was exposed to the influenced of St John of the Cross through his writings. Aspects of Therese's spirituality reflect this, especially when he said, "The soul now realises that all it does for God is flawed and nothing it does is worthy of Almighty God." In her Oblation to Merciful Love, Therese of the Child Jesus echoes his conviction, "When the evening of life comes, I shall stand before Thee with empty hands, because I do not ask Thee, my God, to take account of my works. All our good deeds are blemished in Thine eyes. I wish therefore to be robed with Thine own justice, and to receive for Thy love the everlasting gift of Thyself." Not surprising that Therese would have us put aside any anxiety about our faults and failings, to throw away the scorecards, so to speak and concentrate on loving Jesus with every fibre of our being by exercising sensitivity in order to allow Him to fulfil His need to pour out love upon us. If you feel inclined to spend all night in loving adoration before the Blessed Sacrament, do so, but do it solely to love and physically keep Him company. To offer Him refreshing drinks of pure love but do it before He has time to beg us for a drink, as He had to do with the Samaritan Woman at Jacob's well. Like St Francis of Assisi, Therese experienced a type of affliction on account that Jesus was not loved. She wanted everyone to desire "no other Throne, no other Crown, but Jesus Himself". Not surprising she tells us of her mission on earth and heaven, "Oh, it is love! To love and to be loved and to return to earth to make Love to be loved!"[9]

Love in the heart of the Church

It is conceivable that St. Therese of the Child Jesus, who desired to be 'Love in the heart of the Church' understood Frank Duff to be 'set apart' by the Holy Spirit to mobilise a vast legion of lay people to bring Merciful Love to the world, thus meriting in the heart of the Church, the title 'Father of the lay apostolate.' When one thinks of all the French Marian Saints such as, St. John Eudes, St. Louis Marie De Montfort, St Catherine Laboure of Miraculous Medal fame, St Bernadette of Lourdes and St Therese of Lisieux one could be forgiven for thinking that Our Lady has a predilection for the French Academy of Saints in spreading true devotion to her Immaculate Heart. However, it seems to me that a pattern has emerged, in which DeMontfort, Therese and Frank Duff are the protagonists who take centre stage in

---

[9] 'I am a Daughter of the Church' by Fr. Marie-Eugene, O.C.D. page 622 - St Therese own words. (Novissima Verba) August 10,1897

spreading True Devotion to Mary in the modern world. To make ready a highway for the second coming of the Lord Jesus in Glory. Let us consider the point that St Bernadine of Sienna made: "Every grace which is communicated to this world undergoes a triple process, because it passes from God to Christ, and from Christ through the Virgin is distributed to us." Likewise I see a triple process unfolding in the coming of our 'Three wise men' if you will, namely, St Louis Marie Grignion DeMontfort, St Therese of the Child Jesus and Frank Duff of Dublin. They present at the feet of the people of God 'Gold, Frankincense and Myrrh.'

Gold: A call to Spiritual intimacy with the Blessed Virgin: St. Louis-Marie De Montfort, who as a Catholic Priest stands for Christ the Eternal High Priest, calls for the faithful to renew their baptismal promises by rejecting Satan and all his works, by an act of consecration to the Immaculate Heart of Mary. Thus, our attention is drawn to the Gold of Mary's universal Maternity, thus, echoing our Saviour's exhortation from the Cross: *"Behold your Mother"* (John 19:27)

Frankincense: A call to Spiritual Childhood: St. Therese of the Child Jesus and of the Holy Face, who as a Carmelite nun represents all Religious, presents to the Church the 'Frankincense' of Spiritual Childhood echoing our Saviour's words, *"Unless you become as little children you shall not enter the Kingdom of*

Heaven." (Luke 18:15 -17) *"Whoever is a little one let him come to me."* (Proverbs 9:4)

Myrrh: A universal call to the Laity to engage in the Church's Apostolate: Francis Michael Duff, representing the Laity, presents to the Church the myrrh of the Lay apostolate. At a perilous time in human history he calls the people to arms echoing Our Lord's mandate to each member of His Mystical Body, *"Go throughout the whole world and preach the gospel to all mankind."* (Mark 16:15)

You must find Mary

In stating the above, one does not intend to downplay the role others have played or will play in spreading devotion to the Mother of God. Nor does one imply that our three wise men, so to speak, have fully exhausted the caverns of knowledge concerning the mystery of Mary. That is certainly not the case. However, one has to marvel at the wonderful complementariness of their teachings. Also, one ought to take into consideration that each one of them has left us a spiritual masterpiece. What is absolutely certain is that our protagonists have unequivocally stirred the contemporary conscientiousness of the Church in three key areas. It is also remarkable that both DeMontfort and St. Therese were on a quest for an 'easy way' or elevator to Heaven. St. Louis Marie wrote in his treatise "Everything may be reduced to the search for an **easy way** to obtain from God the grace needed to become a saint; and it is this that I would have you learn. But I say to you that to obtain this grace from God **you must find Mary**." St. Therese echoes De Montfort's sentiments "I've got to take myself just as I am with all my imperfections, but somehow I have to find **a little way,** all my own, which will be a direct short-cut to heaven… Can't I find an elevator which will take me up to Jesus, since I am not big enough to climb the steep stairway of perfection?"

Love is the weight that pulls me forward

Here I want to emphasise that Therese's 'Lift' of spiritual childhood functions perfectly well within the theological superstructure of DeMontfort's True Devotion. Striking indeed is the resemblance in their aspirations. "So it is by Mary that the very little ones are to ascend perfectly and divinely, without fear, to the Most High." (DeMontfort) In his day there were no electric lifts, but he understood the dynamics of lift in the spiritual sense. *"When I am lifted up from the earth, I will draw everyone to me."* (John 12:32) Without the full weight of the Word coming down from heaven at the Incarnation, the dead weight of humanity would remain earthbound. Hence, St. Augustine could say in all truth, "Love is the weight that pulls me forward."

The fact that Love is ever at work and is constantly drawing us to the Father's embrace enhances "the teaching of the Fathers of the Church and among them St Augustine who says that the elect are in the womb of Mary until she brings them forth into the glory of heaven."[10] There can be no doubt that DeMontfort's Marian Theology is entirely congruent with the teaching of St Therese's scripture based doctrine of Spiritual Childhood. Thus, we make the bold discovery, namely, that Mary is God's elevator to Heaven. Therefore, to disassociate ourselves from Mary's maternal mission in our filial response to the Father would be a grave error indeed, "Note that Mary is not only the Mother of Jesus, Head of all the elect, but is also Mother of all his members. Hence, she conceives them, bears them in her womb and brings them forth to the glory of heaven through the graces of God, which she imparts to them." [11]

I will not be able to rest in heaven until the Mystical Body is complete

Although the Servant of God, Frank Duff, has made the Passover to a higher more inclusive dimension, the work of redemption must go on and the Holy Spirit will not release him until the final trumpet sounds. It is

---

[10] DeMontfort's True Devotion to Mary.
[11] Ibid

inconceivable to think that he would be so inebriated with the 'New Wine' that he would fold his arms in blissful repose while his beloved Queen and her Legionaries are hard pressed in establishing the Reign of Christ in all hearts. To Frank Duff we could equally apply the words of St Therese: "I will not be able to rest in heaven until the Mystical Body is complete, until," as she expressed it, "the number of the elect is filled up."[12]

I will spend my heaven in doing good upon earth

I foresee the day when the name of St Therese of the Child Jesus will be invoked with her illustrious compatriot St Louis Marie Grignion DeMontfort along with the other Patrons of the Legion of Mary. That day cannot come too soon as far as I am concern. Shortly before her death Therese said, "I feel that my mission is now to begin, my mission to make others love the good God as I love Him...to give souls my little way. I will spend my heaven in doing good upon earth." The posthumous mission of St Therese will be accomplished through the mediation and in full cooperation of Mary's universal motherhood of souls. Consequently, the Legion of Mary ought to be aligned to her prophetic mission within the Church and seek her powerful intercession by the invocation 'Saint Therese of the Child Jesus and of the Holy Face - pray for us.'

---

[12] 'Where the Spirit Breathes' by Fr. Marie-Eugene OCD page 288 (Alba House – New York)

The though is present to me that when that day comes the Holy Spirit will pour new energy into the Legion of Mary. In a very real way St Therese addresses all those who are on fire with love for Jesus and engaged in the apostolate: "He made me understand these words of the Canticle of Canticles: *"DRAW ME, WE SHALL RUN after you in the odour of your ointments[13]."* O Jesus, it is not even necessary to say: *"When drawing me, draw the souls whom I love!"* The simple statement: "Draw me" suffices; I understand, Lord, that when a soul allows herself to be captivated by the odour of your ointments, she cannot run alone, all the souls whom she loves follow in her train; this is done without constraint, without effort, it is a natural consequence of her attraction for You. Just as a torrent, throwing itself with impetuosity into the ocean, drags after it everything it encounters in its passage, in the same way, O Jesus, the soul who plunges into the shoreless ocean of Your Love, draws with her all the treasures she possesses." (Chapter X1 manuscript C page 254 Story of a Soul) Are not members of the Legion of Mary engaged in the work of drawing others to Jesus as a natural consequence of their union with the Holy Spirit and the Blessed Virgin Mary? I believe when the Legion invokes the intercession of St Therese it will discover that the cause of Frank Duff will speedily advance because there will be no shortage of

---

[13] Canticle of Canticles 1:3

miracles and the Church will become bejewelled with a Legion of little Victims of Merciful Love.

The eyes of the Christian see deep into eternity

I may be accused of prophesising but I am merely acting on intuition. That same intuition that whispers into my consciousness that it is no coincidence that, the Eiffel Tower a civil structure fabricated by human hands during the lifetime of Therese of Lisieux is in fact heaven's intentional tribute to the Theresian 'Lift' of spiritual childhood! To quote another great French mystic St John Vianney: "The eyes of the world see no further than this life. But the eyes of the Christian see deep into eternity". What is the Eiffel Tower but a lift structure par excellence? Majestic it stands dominating the Parisian skyline in the heart of the French Capital, a 19th century masterpiece of civil engineering. Even if you consider my intuition to be false I hope at least you will be prompted the next time you lay eyes on the Eiffel Tower to think about St Therese and her mission to make Love loved in a world that have lost the sense of the Infinite. Following in the example of the Servant of God, Frank Duff I give the final word to St Therese of the Child Jesus and of the Holy Face: "Everyone will see that everything comes from God, any glory that I shall have will be a gratuitous gift from God and will not belong to me. Everybody will see this clearly."

116

Real devotion to Mary obliges apostleship Chapter 5

"To kindle everywhere the fires of divine love – to enlighten those who are in darkness and in the shadow of death – to inflame those who are lukewarm – to bring back life to those who are dead in sin."

In our fast paced high-tech secular society people are finding it hard to maintain a sense of the meaning of life. Thoughts of heaven are seldom brought into the public domain. Huge numbers have abandoned the practise of their Catholic faith. Among the intelligentsia there is much talk of extinction after death, fuelling the philosophy of a stoic existentialism. Christianity is under attack as never before and there is a great deal of confusion regarding religion. In this cultural milieu the Legion of Mary goes out in search of souls to guide them back into the Church so that they may hear the voice of God calling out, 'I Am Who I Am'. [1] At Pentecost the fire of the Holy Spirit fell upon Our Lady and the Apostles. They went out with apostolic zeal to set the known world on fire. With Our Blessed Lady the Servant of God, Frank Duff is calling out to ordinary lay men and women to **"Come along and do this work with**

---

[1] Exodus 3:14

me."[2] Every Christian is called to be a pillar of fire; to be apostolic; it is part and parcel of mystical (hidden) life in Christ. We ought not to miss the opportunity to become saints and luminous signposts for others. We read in the handbook: "The object of the Legion of Mary is the glory of God through the holiness of its members, developed by prayer and active co-operation, under ecclesiastical guidance, in Mary' and the Church's work of crushing the head of the serpent and advancing the reign of Christ."[3]

All said and done, God is Heaven

Frank Duff's relationship with the Holy Spirit and Our Lady alongside his extraordinary love of the Eucharist and deep prayer life indicates his overriding eschatological perspective on life. This statement from him confirms this, "All said and done, God is Heaven. It is His presence which constitutes Heaven."[4] He complained that, "Heaven has no positive attraction for people. It has only the negative attraction that it means escape from Hell. If you look into this position, you will see that it is definitely serious. What should be a tremendous irresistible attraction for the Christian that is the reaping of the reward of his labours, the coming face to face with the Lord and His Mother, and the living with those lovely Persons forever – is not an attraction at

---

[2] Handbook Chapter 10 page 67
[3] Ibid chapter 2 page 11
[4] Mary Shall Reign by Frank Duff chapter 15 page 118

all."[5] He realised that materialism was slowly obfuscating the purpose of human existence. With the Church he wanted to remind people that "The ultimate end of the whole divine economy is the entry of God's creatures into the perfect unity of the Blessed Trinity." (CCC - 260)

As you did it to one of the least members of my family, you did it to me

In the company of Our Lady he contemplated the unfathomable mysteries of God and the salvation of souls. Like St Paul he saw the Church, not as an organisation but an organism with living cells breathing on the mystical wine of Christ. He saw the supreme worth of every individual in the light of their eternal destiny in Christ Jesus and he ordered his whole life around that truth. He wrote about the manner in which one should approach others, "Always will the legionary bear in mind that he is visiting not as a superior to an inferior, not as one equal to another, but as an inferior to his superior, as the servant to the Lord. It is an absence of this spirit that produces the patronising manner." Again "As you did it to one of the least members of my family, you did it to me." His words point directly to the tender words of Jesus in John's Gospel. (Jn14:1-4) *"Do not be worried or upset,"* Jesus told them. *"Believe in God and believe also in me. There are many rooms in my*

---

[5] Ibid chapter 15 page 117

Father's house, and I am going to prepare a place for you. I would not tell you this if it were not so. And after I go and prepare a place for you, I will come back and take you to myself, so that you will be where I am. You know the way that leads to the place where I am going." Frank Duff chose Mary as the 'the way' that leads to Jesus and hence through Jesus to the Eternal Father.

She is an instrument of Divine Mercy

In union with Mary he became one of the great sage Catholic teachers in modern times; a master of spiritual bush craft if you will. Knowing that an organism is one and you cannot separate the head from the body. Like St Paul Frank understood the Church to be Christ. He rigorously held the view that as Mary reigned over every facet of the life of Jesus, the Head of the Mystical Body, so too, she ought to reign over the lives of the rest of the members of His Body. From that perspective Frank acknowledged Mary's divine right to guide all her spiritual children step by step through all the stages of grace to become transformed in Christ. That's really what De Montfort's true devotion to Mary is all about – namely, being transformed in Christ by the Holy Spirit working in each person in the most perfect way possible, namely, in, with and through Mary.

Take everything from her hands

The 'DeMontfort Way' implies falling concretely in love with Our Lady and being involved with her in every facet of her maternal mission and having frequent recourse to her as a child does to its mother. Thus, in the most practical way possible we open ourselves to Mary's maternal care. Another towering Marian mystic of the 20th century and Theologian, St. Maximilian Kolbe made this sweeping statement regarding Our Lady: "Take everything from her hands. Have recourse to her as a child does to its mother. Confide in her. Be concerned about her, for her glory and for the things pertaining to her. Entrust yourself and all things to her care. You must recognise that you have received everything from her, nothing from yourself. All the fruit of your work depends on union with her as she is an instrument of Divine Mercy."

She will make her presence felt in various ways

Frank Duff, founder of the Legion of Mary and St Maximilian Kolbe, founder of the Militia of Mary Immaculate taught that Our Blessed Lady is first and foremost a mother who always knows what is best for each of her children and that she will make her presence felt in various ways. One may not be always aware of Mary's activity in the soul but each person will have a truly unique faith relationship with her. At this stage, it is crucial to understand that true devotion does not consist in being close to her; that is simply not enough. Rather, **true devotion demands intimacy and absolute dependence on her**. One can never repeat too often that intimacy goes hand in hand with dependence on her; in just the same way that Jesus condescended to become a tiny child in the womb of His mother, totally dependent on her even for the very breath of life.

A thick and shapeless tree trunk

A central theme running through De Montfort's Marian theology is the metaphor of the mould. As Eve was created from a rib of Adam, conversely, Christ the New Adam drew His humanity from the 'rib' of Mary so to speak. His Body was perfectly formed in her immaculate womb. In this context, St. Augustine described Mary as the mould of God; an image that St. Louis Marie DeMontfort seized upon and inculcated into his treatise. The idea of a soul being poured into the living mould of Mary so that the fiery touch of the Spirit may faithfully and flawlessly reproduce Jesus Christ, the Prototype Christian, is far more appealing than that of St. Ignatius's image of a soul as, "A thick and shapeless tree trunk"[6] ready to be chiselled into something beautiful by the hand of the sculptor. DeMontfort contended that the safest and least painful way of being transformed into living copies of Jesus Christ is to allow ourselves to be fashioned in the sacred imprint or mould left in Mary's

---

[6] The Heart of Ignatius by Fr. Paul Doncoeur S.J. Helicon Press page 34

womb by God's design. That made sound theological sense to Frank Duff.

Buying the field

The term 'Mary's womb' gives us a better understanding of the meaning of consecration to the Immaculate Heart of Mary. It really is a matter of purchasing the field in order to possess the treasure hidden therein. Christians ought to understand that our act of consecration to Mary is in fact an uncomplicated handing over of our lives to God; it is tantamount to buying the field in order to have the Treasure therein. There really is nothing complicated in loving Jesus and Mary; all shades of mystical union with Our Lady are contingent upon being entirely bound to Christ in mind, body and spirit. Furthermore, we ought to realise that when we place our lives in Mary's hands we simultaneously place them into the hands of the Divine Potter who takes hold of the clay, so to speak, and begins to fashion it into shape. We for our part keep the clay wet and pliable by frequent acts of love towards the Holy Spirit. In this way one is perfectly aligned to receive all the treasures that flow from 'Our Father'.

Stalactite and stalagmite

Now it is time to introduce another mental image. I hope you don't get confused with all these allegories. They are an important means of explaining things of the spirit. I present the soul as a stalagmite. Stalagmites are usually found in caves. The individual growing in grace can be compared to the stalagmite slowly rises upwards from the cave floor by the action of the watery drip calcium tiny salt deposits from the overhanging stalactite. Paradoxically, grace falling from heaven raises us upwards and one happy day a wonderful change will take place when the stalagmite becomes finally fused with the overhanging Stalactite – the transforming union. This is just another allegorical representation of God reaching down and the responsive soul reaching upwards to meet Him in filial union.

The wood begins to char and dry out

This natural process gives us another way of interpreting the 'Transforming union' that St. John of the Cross and St Teresa of Avila spoke about. Again we encounter the Theresian image of the Father reaching down to embrace His 'little child' who so vehemently attempts to reach Him only one is too tiny to negotiate the steep stairway. In regards to human frailty it seems God has developed a stoop. One may ask can a soul on reaching the transforming union grow further in Christ. John of the Cross gives us an affirmative yes to that question in his writings.[7] Even though the stalactite and stalagmite is now connected forming one single column, so to speak, one does not cease to grow in Christ. We are constantly being fleshed out from one degree of glory to another; the so called *many mansions*. Again one becomes lost

---

[7] The Living Flame of Love

for words and has to communicate by means of imagery. We fall back on John of the Cross's analogue of the log placed in the fire to describe growth in God. Placed in the fire the wood begins to char and dry out and as it gets hotter and hotter it catches fire and as the flames slowly eat into the log it becomes one with the flames. So too a soul with all its imperfections is consumed in the Living Flame of Love - divinized.

The man who thus makes the Holy Spirit his helper enters into the tide of omnipotence

It is within the context of the 'transforming union' that I situate Frank Duff's contemplative relationship with the Holy Spirit and Our Lady. Hence he makes this very important point:

"The man who thus makes the Holy Spirit his helper enters into the tide of omnipotence. If one of the conditions for so attracting Him is the understanding of Our Lady's relation to Him, another vital condition is that we appreciate the Holy Spirit Himself as a real, distinct, Divine Person with His appropriate mission in regards to us. This appreciation of Him will not be maintained except there be a reasonably frequent turning of the mind to Him. By including just that glance in His direction, every devotion to the Blessed Virgin can be made a wide-open way to the Holy Spirit." [8]

---

[8] Walking with Mary - Article 14, The Legionary and the Holy Trinity.

There is a basic reason why the Catholic Church may never cease to be apostolically active. Since a flame is always active generating light and heat, so too the Church guided by the Holy Spirit must always be generating the Light of Christ and the warmth of His love. From that perspective Frank Duff held the view that love for the Holy Spirit and devotion to Our Lady are of necessity authenticated by being apostolically active. Since Vatican II the Magisterium has stressed: "On all the laity, then, falls the glorious burden of toiling to bring the divine offer of salvation ever more into reach of all men of all times and all over the world. They must have every path opened to a whole-hearted personal participation, and their strength and the needs of the time allow, in the saving work of the Church."[9] In our relationship with God, again and again we come across the need for people to be actively involved in the apostolate.

Streams of Life-giving Water

In the Gospel of John, Jesus spoke of a highpoint in our relationship with Him when He said: *"Whoever loves me will obey my teaching. My Father will love him, and my Father and I will come to him, and will live with him".* *(John 14:23)* One does not imply that each person will have the same empirical experience of the activity of the Blessed Trinity present in the soul. However, each

---

[9] Lumen Gentium 33

person will experience in some measure what Jesus referred to as *"Streams of Life-giving Water"[10]* flowing out from within him and establishing an unearthly peace and joy causing the individual to sing out with the Psalmist: *"With my whole being I sing for joy to the living God."[11]* This is what the Apostle Paul experienced when he said: *"I am running over with joy"[12]* or with St Peter *"Rejoice with a great joy which words cannot express, because you are receiving the salvation of your souls, which is the purpose of your faith in him."[13]* In the watershed of the transforming union supernatural joy is a manifestation of the Trinitarian presence and the human condition can hardly contain it. Edel Quinn's friend Mary Walls remarked, "She spoke most frequently about the indwelling of the Blessed Trinity in the soul."[14]

Love is dwelling within us at every moment of the day and night

Shortly before her death the Carmelite St. Elizabeth of the Trinity said: **"I confide to the secret of which has made my life an anticipated heaven: the belief that a Being Whose name is Love is dwelling within us at every moment of the day and night and that He asks us to live in His company."[15]** A consequence of entering into a deeper relationship with God is that one's

---

[10] John 7:37 -39
[11] Psalm 84 verse 2
[12] 2 Cor 7:4
[13] 1Peter 8:9
[14] The First Edel – by Fr. Brain McKevitt OP
[15] Letter 34

faith gaze on Jesus and Mary becomes hypersensitive or contemplative. Like the aroma of tasty food one is filled with the eschatological presentiment of the beautiful wedding garment Our Lady is preparing for her child. In this regard St Elizabeth of the Trinity tells us, "It is she, the Immaculate Conception, who gave me the habit of Carmel, and I am asking her to clothe me again in that robe of fine linen in which the bride is decked to present herself at the marriage feast of the Lamb."[16]

We must have the mind of Christ

The Holy Spirit leads us on a higher path therefore Christians ought to constantly repeat with Paul: *"It is no longer I who live ...but it is Christ who lives in me."*[17] (Gal 2:20) In the Spirit the Christian encounters Christ from within. That is why Frank Duff who was entirely Christocentric in his thinking was fond of quoting *"We must have the mind of Christ."*[18] Another great mystic pointed out: "The soul is completely illuminated by the Holy Spirit. And thus, seeing with the mind the desirable and only ineffable beauty, such a person is pierced with divine passionate love and is directed in the way of all values of the Spirit."[19]

---

[16] Letter 29 from the year 1906

[17] See Legion Handbook 'Basic duties of Legionaries' – Ch 33, section 13

[18] 1 Corinthians 2:16

[19] Pseudo-Macarius (c390) was an Egyptian monk and hermit - Magnificat June edition 2012 page 108

It was with the mind of Jesus Christ that Frank fathomed the inestimable worth of the human person. An atheist/scientist may only consider his fellow man to be little more that 72% water and 28% matter. In his essay entitled "Thinking in Christ"[20] Frank Duff echoes Paul's teaching when he quotes: "The Christian," says Olier, "is properly speaking Jesus Christ living in man." The Apostle to the Gentiles envisioned himself and everybody else living in God as in a vast ocean like space[21] for he says: *"In him we live and move and have our being."*[22] Frank Duff saw that space to be the theatre of Mary's maternal operations. In other words, he saw the manifold apostolate of the Church within the context of Mary's Spiritual Maternity and he saw them as one inseparable movement. He understood that to engage in any kind of apostolate without Mary would be contrary to the divine plan and tantamount to gathering leaves in a storm.

It is not good for Man to be alone

It may be said that union with Mary is mysteriously tied up in that passage from Genesis 2:18 - *"It is not good for Man to be alone; I will give him a helper who will be like him."* In the divine scheme of things that 'helper'

---

[20] Thinking in Christ now available in volume 1 'Gems of Wisdom' page 46 & 51

[21] 1 Cor 12:27

[22] Acts 17:28

would have to be someone untainted by the effects of the Fall - a New Eve. That New Eve is Mary the Mother of the Saviour who now enjoys the beatific vision. In Mary there is a glorious synergy of the finite and the Infinite. To her I apply the words of sacred scripture: *"Send her forth from your holy heaven...that she may be with me and work with me that I may know your pleasure."* (Wisdom 9:10) The Church directs our attention to Mary as that great eschatological sign, the portent of the Book of Revelation 12: 1. "The Assumption of the Blessed Virgin is a singular participation in her Son's Resurrection and an anticipation of the resurrection of the other Christians."[23]

Burning bush

I am fond of the imagery that scripture presents of the 'Burning bush' in describing the ineffable union of God with the human family. Have you ever observed the bluish glow within a bright red flame? As John of the Cross indicates we are the oxygen burning within the Trinitarian Flames. The members of Christ's Mystical Body are the authentic 'Burning Bush' that Moses saw in the wilderness of Sinai. Moses sent by God to free the Israelites from the Egyptians was himself a Messianic prefiguring of the Messiah who would come in a new moment in human history to cast fire upon the earth.[24] In

---

[23] CCC 966
[24] Luke 12:49

this Uncreated Fire we can say with St Paul all the baptised live and move and have their being. Truly man is destined to burn forever in the fire of Merciful Love. Just as the old Adam brought death, Christ the New Adam casts upon humanity the fire of indestructibility.[25]

The full content of divine nature lives in Christ

Post resurrection Jesus has not dissolved back into the single nature of Spirit; all our hope is contingent on his sacred humanity. Jesus Christ remains forever a human being, a God-Man. As St Paul points out: *"The full content of divine nature lives in Christ, in his humanity, and you have been given full life in union with him."*[26] That's the Good News that Christ exhorted his Apostles to preach.[27] It is precisely for that purpose the Legion of Mary came into existence; "to kindle everywhere the fires of divine love – to enlighten those who are in darkness and in the shadow of death – to inflame those who are lukewarm – to bring back life to those who are dead in sin."[28]

May your love be my life within me

We are again struck by the constant references to fire. We find this quotation from St Augustine in the True

---

[25] CCC 1025
[26] Col 2:9
[27] Mark 16:15
[28] Concluding prayer on the Legion of Mary prayer card.

Devotion to Mary. "Now from this time forth, do ye, all my desires, grow hot, and flow out upon the Lord Jesus. O sweet Jesus may every good feeling that is fitted for your praise, love you, delight in you, adore you! God of my heart and my portion, Christ Jesus, may my heart faint away in spirit, and may your love be my life within me! May the live coal of your love grow hot within my spirit and break forth into a perfect fire; may it burn incessantly on the altar of my heart; may it glow in my innermost being; may it blaze in the hidden recesses of my soul; and in the days of my consummation may I be found consummated with Thee! Amen." This prayer from the burning heart of Augustine adds more weight to Our Saviour's words. *"I have come to set the earth on fire, and how I wish it were already kindled."*

The system of the Legion of Mary is a most excellent one

Frank Duff was another man on fire with the Holy Spirit. He was another Patrick, someone who has not just heard the voice of the Irish but the voice of the whole of world calling out to him; he is an apostle to all humanity. He wrote "The fact that God in His Providence has left us in the world, instead of giving us a religious vocation, indicates that He wishes the world to be our vocation." [29] That's just the way Frank saw it. Yet, he knew this could only be done by each individual pouring himself into another soul. That is the modus operandi of the Legion of Mary, namely, the person to person approach.

---

[29] See Can We be Saints – page 30

Under Mary's direction Frank Duff 'grew beneath her touch' to use his own expression. Union with her was a crucial ingredient in his mystical life. Every fibre of his being was cross-stitched with love for Our Lady. It overflowed into the nitty-gritty of every facet of his natural and supernatural life. His was no hermitically sealed self-contained private devotion; rather his devotion to Mary transcended all forms of personalism. For him to serve Mary was both a duty and an honour. Jesus and Mary was the object of all his actions. In that sense one could never abstract him from the mission of the Church *"Go throughout the whole world and preach the gospel to all people."(Mark 16:15)*. In fact it would be difficult to conjure up images of him without some association with the apostolic organisation he founded.

The Legion wants to offer her a practical possibility of exercising that motherly function

Miss Hilda Firtel, a Legion envoy working in Germany just after World War II, while addressing a gathering of 60 priests gave them the Legion's perspective on Mary:

"The Legion's Mariology rests on one central idea. Mary was the mother of Jesus Christ whom she nourished and served during his earthly life. On Golgotha, beneath the Cross, she became the Mother of Men; and since then she has been bestowing the same motherly care on the mystical Christ, namely the Church. The Legion wants to offer her a practical possibility of exercising that motherly function; it seeks to identify itself with Mary and tries to see in every human being the person of Our Lord, who must be loved and served."

Near the close of her address the Bishop entered the assembly hall and said to her "Please continue". When Hilda concluded her talk she held her breath. She knew one deflationary remark from His Excellency could undo all her efforts to promote the Legion in Germany. Bishop Weskamm then spoke to the assembly of Priests: "Reverend Fathers", he began, "I have to admit that in the beginning I had been apprehensive about the Mariology of the Legion. But I am convinced that this Mariology is the soundest, the most beautiful, in fact the only correct and complete one, because it takes into account the role of Our Lady in the divine plan, and on the other hand preserves us from purely sentimental devotion."[30] It must be noted that what Miss Firtel said of the Legion of Mary comes from the heart of its founder.

Drenched in the blood of four thousand martyrs

Nowadays it seems there is no shortage of liberal thinking individuals who regard the Legion of Mary as an anachronism maintaining that it has run its course.

---

[30] Conquest for Mary – by Hilda Firtel pages 158 &159 Clonmore & Reynolds Ltd. London: Burns & Oats Ltd

Such people display monumental ignorance. Far from withering on the vine the Legion of Mary has come into its own and is uniquely equipped to the task of combating the secular culture of the 21st Century. Already the Legion is drenched in the blood of some four thousand martyrs who met their death at the hands of the Chinese Communists. Legionary priests were imprisoned, tortured and killed; many Legionary teenagers sent to prison did not get out again until they were in their forty's. Furthermore the Legion has given the Church a new breed of saint; some of whom are the rarest flowers ever to appear on the mystical vine. The vast majority of them will never wear the canonical crown of sainthood. It is truly remarkable that everywhere in the ranks of the Legion one will encounter heroic sanctity.

Real devotion to Mary obliges apostleship

Under the watching eye of Frank Duff the Legion of Mary grew organically from within the Catholic Church. It has given the Church an immense army to say the rosary[31]and it has played a pivotal role in cracking wide open the unhealthy orthodoxy that was prevalent in the minds of the majority of clergy and laity alike in the early half of the 20th century. Frank Duff's robust theological thinking challenged the mindset that sequestered the layperson to a non-combatant zone of

---

[31] See Handbook of the Legion of Mary page 146

Church Militant. In a country well stocked with Seminarians, Priests and Religious with large church attendances, he began to build the apostolic ark of the Legion of Mary by training the laity into tenacious foot soldiers of Mary Immaculate. Many laughed at him but Frank reiterated "Real devotion to Mary obliges apostleship.[32]"

The Legion of Mary presents the true face of the Catholic Church

Like Noah of old, Frank Duff was given a hard time by people in high and low ecclesial places. Yet, how remarkable wherever the Ark of the Legion comes into port it breaks open the pure nard of Catholicism spreading its sacred spores everywhere; Christianity is put into practice. Contrary to what some individuals think, there is nothing in its makeup that is extraneous to placing the feet of Christ firmly on the footstool of Creation. That is why it has weathered every storm and criticism and claimed the admiration of every Pope since its foundation. By challenging and educating the laity as to their true place in the life of the Church, Frank Duff has effectively heralded in a new apostolic era in keeping with the 'New Marian Age'. He thus initiated a long called for paradigm shift that has greatly contributed to power-cleaning the face of Catholic orthodoxy and has effectively dismantled the old paradigm of private devotion to Mary.

---

[32] Handbook ,Chapter 6, section 3

By inscribing the Old Testament image of the 'Pillar of Fire' into the structure of the Legion of Mary, Mr Duff has created its unique leitmotif or identity badge by linking Our Lady with the work of the Holy Spirit. He too sees Mary as the 'Woman of Genesis' symbolically represented as the 'Pillar of Fire', who will lead all God's children through that triumphant arch at the rainbows end where time evanesces into eternity. That eschatological image is seen on the cover of every Legion handbook and it adorns the 'Tessera' or prayer card which contains the official Legion prayers.[33] The biblical image of Mary 'Pillar of fire' is framed by that victorious passage from Genesis 3:15 when God addresses Satan, *"I will put enmity between you and the woman, and between your offspring and hers; she will strike your head."* In chapter 25 of the handbook you will read this telling quotation from St. Alphonsus Liguori Doctor of the Church, "In the Old Testament we read that the Lord conducted his people from Egypt to the land of promise, *'by day in a pillar of cloud and by night in a pillar of fire.'* (Ex 13:21) This stupendous pillar, at one time of cloud and at another of fire was a figure of Mary and of the various offices which she performs on our behalf."

---

[33] See chapter 25 and 26 of the Legion Handbook

One is reminded of Our Lady's words to Sister Lucia: "My Immaculate Heart will be your refuge." Throughout his life the Servant of God laboured to corral souls beneath the safety of the 'Cloud' or 'Pillar' of Mary's maternal care. At Fatima Our Lady gave the world a reminder of that biblical analogue when she came at a perilous moment in history on a cloud to visit little Jacinta, Francisco and Lucia in order to rain down graces upon humanity. As scripture says[34], *"When you see a cloud coming up in the west, at once you say that it is going to rain and it does."* Equally we may say wherever there is grace, there is the Holy Spirit and wherever there is the Holy Spirit, there is Mary.

---

[34] Luke 15:54 "When you see a cloud coming up in the west, at once you say that it is going to rain- and it does."

To Flower in Mary

Chapter 6

I am the vine and you are the branches. Those who remain in me, and I in them will bear much fruit; for you can do nothing without me. - John 15:5

While waiting among the pilgrims for the final boarding call for our flight back to Dublin, I had the honour of Rev. Fr. Bede McGregor, procurator of the cause of Frank Duff, taking the empty seat beside me. Later, I could not help thinking that just like Frank Duff's interior life there was more to Lourdes than meets the eye. As the aircraft tore down the runway and booted up into the open sky, my mind flooded with thoughts. I sensed that Lourdes ushered in a paradigm shift, to use a philosophical term, a new way of interpreting devotion to Our Lady entirely consonant with the teaching of St Louis Marie Grignion DeMontfort. I felt that Lourdes was a call to spiritual intimacy with Our Lady; a call that was simply not heard. I realised that if I was to get any peace I would have to transcribe some of my impressions on paper. Although the events of Lourdes are well documented and authenticated, nevertheless, for some time I have felt that an important narrative had been overlooked. Essentially, there has been a failure to interpret a vital sign given by the Mother of God at the

139

shrine. In this chapter I hope to highlight the missing narrative.

Sacred Scripture is replete with signs and symbols. Indeed the final book of Scripture, the Book of Revelation is a veritable semiotic goldmine. The Cross itself is a semiotic symbol of mankind's ultimate freedom. The Godless Communists tried to replace it with the 'Hammer and Sickle' and secular society seems bent on having it banished from the public square. Most significant is the fact that the very first sign Our Lady gave to St Bernadette was the sign of the Cross. One is not surprised at this because "The Cross is the superabundance of God's love poured out upon this world."[1] Afterwards Bernadette was admired for the remarkable way she made it in imitation of Our Lady

A caged bird

From a psychological point of view it is good to go on a pilgrimage because at times the soul feels like a caged bird or one who has had its primary feathers damaged. Since the ability to fly is inscribed by the Creator into the nature of a bird and although it cannot fly away, it never loses the innate aptitude to fly and the memory of flight is always present. Similarly, since the 'Fall'

---

[1] John Paul II - Vita consecrata n 24

humankind has had its primary feathers cut, if you will, and is therefore grounded and limited. However, unlike the little bird, even in perfect freedom, we will not be satisfied until we discover within ourselves the dormant ability to fly on the wings of faith and prayer, high above the clouds of mere instinct and sensibility. To commune with God who has inscribed in every human heart the capacity for love and fellowship with Himself. To love God is as natural as a bird singing, a dog barking or a baby crying.

Innate homing device

Without a relationship with God we lose a sense of our own identity and place in the cosmic scheme of creation. From that point of view it is understandable that all religions, whether ancient or contemporary, have their own particular strain of mysticism. But mysticism, whether Catholic or otherwise, is just a euphemism that underpins that innate homing device in every human heart that seeks to make direct contact with 'Uncreated Wisdom'. In one sense Man can be compared to a person who has lost an arm in an accident whereby the phantom arm causes real pain in the psyche. Going on a pilgrimage is one rational response to that phantom pain deep within the human heart; it is tantamount to going to the hills when the heart is lonely[2].

---

[2] The Sound of Music film

At the grotto a poverty stricken teenager, Bernadette Soubirous, at times acts out unknowingly the part of the Blessed Virgin Mary, who herself had to eat the bitter herb and drink from the bitter chalice so that humanity could freely drink from the crystal spring of salvation that flows from the wounded Heart of the Redeemer. Bernadette's 'yes' to Our Lady is an echo of Mary's 'Fiat' which initiated the Biggest Bang in the universe when Spirit entered time, space and matter. There fell from Heaven the subatomic 'God Particle' (Christ) into Mary's womb that would grow to maturity and bind all humanity together, thus generating in time the Church - the Mystical Body of Christ. It is a wise person who understands that true mysticism begins at the feet of Mary because there lies hidden the authentic spring of union with God. That may be one reason why Lourdes is unique among Marian Shrines and it is the only place Our Lady requested people to go to. "Go tell priests that people are to come here in procession and to build a chapel here." History will testify that Our Lady's request was prudential.

Hidden from sight

Over the years Lourdes has exercised an unexplainable power to rehabilitate the human condition, spiritually, mentally and physically; all shades of brokenness. You will discover that it is an exciting place full of mystery where the miraculous is on tap demonstrating the active presence of the Most Holy Spirit. The word mystery implies something hidden from sight that is only revealed by faith and in many ways Lourdes fits that description. There is more to Lourdes than meets the eye and each person who goes there on pilgrimage will have their own individual faith tale to tell. Let me share with you one of my experiences.

Press-ganged into compliance

Some years ago on a sunny afternoon at the Lourdes Lake which is situated just above the town not far from Bartres, where Saint Bernadette looked after the sheep, a middle-aged Priest shared his account of his first pilgrimage to Lourdes with myself and my wife. With the simplicity of a child he told us his story as we sat dangling our bare feet from the little wooden jetty into the cool water. He explained that he was a late vocation and had just been appointed curate in a new parish, when he found himself elevated to the status of spiritual director to a highly organised group of seasoned pilgrim goers to Lourdes. On arrival, after the long journey by train, plane and bus he thought he would quietly retire and get a good night's rest. Wrong! The group had other plans. "We're meeting in the lobby at 11:45pm to go down to the Grotto, its tradition," he was told. He remonstrated with them, but to no avail. Overruled he was press-ganged into compliance and he was frogmarched to the Grotto in the main sanctuary.

In the cool midnight air he sat praying with the group in the flickering glow of candlelight. Then he began to think, "What on earth am I doing here hundreds of kilometres from home sitting praying before a stone statue?" In disgust he up stakes and made his way back to the hotel without uttering a word to anyone. However, all changed the very next day. While sitting among the multilingual crowd at the Grotto a deep peace began to invade his whole being, lifting his spirits and filling him with a new kind of inner calm and joy. For the rest of his pilgrimage he was in sync with his parish group. The end result was his stay in Lourdes was enormously rewarding; he became so attracted to the grotto that he found it hard to leave it. At the end tears flowed as the group made their customary farewell visit to the Grotto. That story is typical of many people who go there for the first time. How reassuring to see all the different nationalities that make up the Mystical Body pausing reverently to pray at the Grotto, walking and singing in the processions.

Pray at the feet of Our Lady

What is it about Lourdes that leaves such lasting impressions in the soft tissue of the consciousness as we begin to notice the benefits of coming to pray at the feet of Our Lady? Back home subtle changes take place causing some to reflect that their fuse to anger seems to burn a lot slower than before; they even begin to make excuses for the various tonalities of Adam's weaknesses in others. They get a sense that they are more human, compassionate and less self-centred; they feel less tense and laugh more. Life seems more meaningful and their participation at Mass is more reverent. Many discover or rediscover the power of reciting the rosary and praying before the Blessed Sacrament. A pilgrimage strengthens our Catholic faith and prepares us to meet life's challenges and helps us appreciate why the Church instructs, "Let the entire body of the faithful pour forth perseveringly prayer to the Mother of God and Mother of all people."[3] To realise that Mary is truly a gift from God, "A gift from which Christ himself makes personally to every individual."[4] The call to intimacy with Mary comes directly from the mouth of Jesus, Who when suffocating on the Cross addressed His Mother with torturous breathes, *"Here is your son."* *Then he said to the disciple, "She is your mother."* (John 19: 26-27) In doing so, Jesus is expressing the Will of His Father. When we undertake True devotion to Mary we open our hands to accept all the treasure of God's Mercy. We let the genie out of the box, if you will, and become overwhelmed by all sorts of serendipitous wonders that flow through Mary the Treasurer of Divine Mercy.

---

[3] Lumen Gentium, n.69
[4] Redemptoris Mater – John Paul II page 61 section 45.

One is reminded of St. Paul urging the Church at Ephesus to wear "truth as a belt/girdle around your waist"[5]. Perhaps this might explain why Our Lady wore a blue girdle around her waist at Lourdes when she affirmed the Dogmatic Truth of her Immaculate Conception. Mary is the Mother of Eternal (Jesus Christ) Truth and if truth had a colour, I imagine it to be blue. Our Lady's eyes may not be blue, but I believe people are correct to assume her eyes are blue because Mary reflects Truth as calm limpid alpine waters reflect a clear blue sky above. Whenever I hear that lovely Song, 'The Rose of Tralee,' I am reminded of this truth. **'She is lovely and fair as the rose of summer, but it was not her beauty that won my heart – it was the Truth in her eyes ever dawning, that made me love Mary ...'**. In line with the teaching of DeMontfort one would also be correct to assume that Frank's contemplative gaze on truth was through the eyes of Our Lady who lives within the intense glow of 'unapproachable Light.'

He must increase, but I must decrease

Although we cannot add to God's omnipotence, God desires us to grow in Him. Paradoxically, Jesus calls humanity to intimacy with His Blessed Mother in order for humanity to decrease. Therefore it is good psychology to put into practise the maxim of John the

---

[5] Ephesians 6:14

Baptist. *"He must increase, but I must decrease."* (John 3:30) That seems so counterintuitive, but really when you analyse it; to decrease in order to increase in grace is the secret of holiness. To be drawn into intimacy with Our Lady is to imitate the Redeemer who allowed Himself to decrease in Mary at the incarnation. Could one exercise a greater intimacy with Mary than that? Coming to the feet of Our Lady we bow so low: Oh! To be raised so high.

Non-contingent ground of contingency

Furthermore, we ought to bear in mind that Jesus, the second Person of the Blessed Trinity is God and therefore has no need of anything in all creation including the Blessed Virgin Mary. Jesus is the Eternal Word, 'the non-contingent ground of contingency' who is consubstantial with the Father and the Holy Spirit; He is absolutely sufficient unto to Himself. This truth helps us grasp the mystery of God's plan of salvation and thus we begin to see Mary as that luminous constant where divinity and humanity have harmoniously come together. In Mary we experience the wonders of God's Merciful Love and rest easy in the knowledge that there exists in the divine mind an excellent reason for Mary's maternal mission in the world. The Mother of Jesus is uniquely interwoven into the fabric of Christianity and in the pages of the biblical narrative from start to finish.

In 1858 at Lourdes the curtain separating heaven and earth was drawn 18 times during the heavenly drama played out on the stage at the rock of Massabielle from the 11th February to the closing act on the 16th July, the feast of Our Lady Mount Carmel. The drama was initiated by a gust of wind "I heard in the brambles a noise like a gust of wind." A sound that caught Bernadette's attention and caused her to look in the direction of the niche which is about 10 feet above the ground, there she saw a young Lady bathed in an unearthly light. Bernadette was quick to notice that the gust of wind did not disturb the tall poplar trees along the Gave River. Some writers have made a comparison with the 'wind' that registered the coming of the Holy Spirit at Pentecost. [6] However, it is true to say that at the feet of Our Lady there is always a 'gust of wind', that is to say, the activity of the Divine Pneuma, the Holy Spirit. It is the Spirit who reinvigorates, empowers and fixes one's gaze permanently on the horizon of Heaven.

Sparks shooting up from a log fire

It seems that Our Lady's coming and going from heaven has trapped within our atmosphere a heavenly ambience that lingers in the vicinity of the apparition site. Praying there one gets a real sense that the gap between heaven and earth is very tenuous. So tenuous in fact, as to leave

---

[6] Hebrews 12:26 - 27

the impression that what separates us from God is as thin as the watery edge of a soap bubble. Indeed, one gets the impression that earth is a bubble universe within the incomprehensible expanse of eternity. A trumpet blast, a sudden burst and time will vanish in the blink of an eye and all things will be made new. Over the years Jesus and Mary have appeared many times to certain people, however, strictly speaking they do not appear to anybody. Rather it is a dispensation imputed to the individual in order to fulfil a particular purpose as was the case with St. Paul on the Damascus road and Moses in the Desert. The same is true of Saint Juan Diego, St Bernadette and the children at Fatima when they were given the extraordinary privilege of speaking face to face with the Mother of Jesus. Although Jesus and Mary exist outside of time they are incredibly close to us at all times. Our Lady and the holy Angels constantly see us and God at the same time. One gets the impression they effortlessly move in and out of our dimension quicker than sparks shooting up from a log fire.

My Dove, hiding in the clefts of the rock

To help us on our life's pilgrimage it seems that God has thought of everything and left nothing to chance. Although that 'everything' may not always be within the scope of human understanding, for as St. Paul exclaimed, *"O the depth of the riches and wisdom and knowledge of God! How unsearchable are his judgements and how inscrutable his ways! "For who has known the mind of the Lord or who has been his counsellor?"'* (Romans 11: 33-34) The grace of the Immaculate Conception which Mary received at the moment of her conception redounds to the whole human family. Looking upon her image at the grotto one may experience an eschatological epiphany, seeing in that image of Our Lady we get a glimpse of the whole of humanity bathed in the Glory of God, made holy by the sacrifice of the Lamb – washed immaculate in His Blood.[7] In gratitude we cry out to Our Lady *"My Dove, hiding in the clefts of the rock, in the coverts of the cliff, show me your face, let me hear your voice, for your voice is sweet and your face is lovely."* (Song of Songs poem 2 verse 14)

Immaculate protection

Without directly referring to the Church's proclamation of the Dogma of the Immaculate Conception in 1854 Our Lady in 1858 gave her approval to this dogma by plainly stating to St Bernadette "I am the Immaculate Conception". Within the mystery of the Incarnation, Mary is our 'Immaculate **protection**' against Satan. In Mary there is always an incompatibility between light and darkness[8] and that no infernal monkeys (devils) may ever cross the threshold of this Cathedral of Light. As Christians, we constantly have to make moral judgements in order to be one step ahead of Satan who is

---

[7] Isaiah 53:5
[88] Genesis 3:15 "I will put enmity between you and the woman....."

our deadly enemy. *"So the dragon was furious with the woman and left to wage war against the rest of her offspring – those who keep the commandments of God and have the testimony about Jesus."*[9] St Paul was very aware of the spiritual warfare going on all around him and he warned the Church in Ephesus: *"For it is not against human enemies that we have to struggle, but against the principalities and the ruling forces who are masters of the darkness in this world, the spirits of evil in the heavens."* [10] In the very first chapter of the Legion handbook you will read a quotation from Vatican II[11], "The whole life of men, both individual and social, shows itself to be a struggle, and a dramatic one, between good and evil, between light and darkness."

Dark matter

Notwithstanding that Christ alone has overcome Satan by His death on the Cross and His rising from the dead we are nonetheless obliged to take into consideration the constant danger posed by the 'Dark matter' of sin generated by that fallen star Lucifer. This 'dark matter' so to speak, has the power to destroy the light of Christ in every individual. Then factor in the weaknesses inherent in the human condition that Paul talks about in Romans[12]and you have compelling reasons to put on the panoply, that is to say, the full armour of Mary's

---

[9] Revelation 12:17
[10] Ephesians 6:12
[11] Gaudium et Spes
[12] Romans 7:14 - 25

protection. This helps us grasp the metaphysical power of the medal that is called the Miraculous Medal and the prayer that Our Lady gave to St Catherine Laboure in 1830 in Paris. "O Mary, conceived without sin, pray for us who have recourse to thee." This prayer coined in heaven may be seen on every Legion of Mary standard or Vexillium as it is known. The Miraculous Medal when blessed by a Priest and worn around the neck has inexplicable power over Satan.

She is once, twice, three times Our Lady

Lest we forget Mary's relationship with the Trinity, one may barrow the words of the song made popular by Lionel Richie, "She is once, twice, three times Our Lady" because as Daughter of the Father and Mother of the Redeemer, she constantly draws from the Fountain of Mercy that flows from the Sacred Heart of Jesus through His Holy Spirit, her Spouse. Uzzah,[13] the son of Abinadad, died when he reached out and touched the Ark of the Covenant. This may seem very cruel and cause some to see God as a cold hearted law enforcer; nothing could be further from the truth. In this narrative we catch a glimpse of the nature of God who is love. Jesus acted like Uzzah; he reached out to humanity at the cost of his own life. At the time the people of Israel were subject to the old Law. But with the revelation of God becoming man, the old law has been swallowed up in the New Covenant of the Blood of Jesus Christ. Effectively

---

[13] The second book of Samuel 6:6

Jesus has caught fallen humanity in an eternal embrace. Mankind is no longer subject to the old law; man is freed from the consequences of the fall which is eternal separation from God. Paradoxically, human freedom is contingent on our reaching out and touching the New Art of the Covenant. O the wonder of it all! Don't you see that by reaching out to Mary the living Ark of the New Covenant we invariably make contact with the Son of God and live? Devotion to Mary ought to be seen from that point of view. Mary is the first Monstrance that contains the Author of Eternal Life! A thought we ought to have foremost in our minds when at Lourdes during the Eucharistic procession or in adoration before the Blessed Sacrament.

Do you know what the roses meant?

The herald of the coming Age of Mary, St Louis Marie-Grignion De Montfort in his treatise on 'true devotion' makes the distinction between true devotion to Mary and imperfect devotion to her. Like a lovesick horticulturist DeMontfort sought to gather all the beautiful flowers in all creation, that is to say, every precious soul and present them at the feet of the Queen of Heaven. Through his writings he is still gathering souls at the feet of Mary. In a remarkable way Our Lady of Lourdes has tacitly endorsed DeMontfort's universal call to consecration to her Immaculate Heart long years before the events of Fatima. Once again I draw your attention to the feet on the image of Our Lady of Lourdes. What do you see? Yes, a yellow rose on each foot! To this day people have wondered about the true significance; even our heroine St. Bernadette did not understand their true meaning. When she was questioned by Father Corbin[14] "Do you know what the roses meant?" She replied, "No Monsieur."

I do not desire closeness, I desire intimacy

One may not assume that Our Lady was demonstrating the latest fashion the citizens of heaven were wearing at that time. Of course the roses are semiotic, that is to say, they have meaning. However, to this day no one seems to have uncovered their true meaning. Some 16 years ago I got the answer to that question by way of a strange phenomenon called an 'interior locution'. I was standing directly beneath the apparition site at the Grotto when I experienced a voice reverberating within me saying "I do not desire closeness, I desire intimacy." Consequently, I understood Our Lady was expressing her predilection for the primacy of intimacy as opposed to being close to her. In other words DeMontfort had got it right! He understood that 'True devotion' flourishes when one becomes intimate with Mary.

Mystical Rose tree

Now let's consider the events of 1858 when a perplexed Fr. Peyramale, the Parish Priest of Lourdes at the time of the apparitions had asked Bernadette to request the

---

[14] Bernadette Speaks – by Rene Laurentin page 200

unknown Lady "to make the wild roses bloom." There was a rosebush on the site of the apparitions at the time, and still is today. The P.P. wanted a miraculous sign; heaven's confirmation if you will that it was the Blessed Virgin Mary appearing at the grotto at Massabielle. It's very probable that Fr. Peyramale had in mind the miraculous happenings at Guadalupe in 1531, when Our Lady appearing to St. Juan Diego performed the requested miracle (of roses) for Bishop Zummarraga of Mexico. At Lourdes things were very different. Peyramale had no idea that his request on this occasion was the most inappropriate one he could possibly have made. The reason being is that Our Lady was allegorically representing herself to the whole world as the Mystical Rose tree, which of course is perennially in bloom regardless of the seasons. That's why Our Lady was wearing a yellow rose on each bare foot; a reference to intimacy and union. In an eschatological sense the colour yellow is a reference to the perpetual springtime that occurs within the life of the soul at the moment of baptism. At baptism one is grafted onto the Tree of Life; transferred from the kingdom of darkness to the Kingdom of Light. Christians must never forget that Light (Jesus Christ) came from heaven through the prism of Mary's Immaculate Heart. Since then nothing in the order of grace has changed.

Wild brambles

The 'wild brambles' at the base of the niche of the apparitions are representative of being close to Mary, but **not intimate** with her. Being close to Mary, means we are free to grow independent of her maternal influence, we are still calling the shots, so to speak. There is a substantial difference between being close to Mary and being intimate with her; they are two very different ontological relationships. True devotion as taught by De Montfort demands the intimacy of an absolute dependence on her as depicted by the yellow roses on her feet as if growing out of her very person. To this day you will see at the Grotto two symbols representing devotion to Mary, one true, the other imperfect. One depicted in marble, and the other growing naturally beneath her image. One is not implying that Our Lady is in some way less attentive to individuals who have a not so perfect relationship with her. However, according to DeMontfort the practise of true devotion to Mary allows her greater latitude to bring us into a deeper relationship with her Son and the Holy Spirit. Under Mary's intimate maternal touch we are best calibrated to the rhythm of life in the Blessed Trinity.

I am the Immaculate Conception

The reality is that if Our Lady had made the wild roses bloom out of season, it would have undone the semiotic meaning of the yellow roses worn on her feet and thereby given her sanction to an imperfect relationship with souls. To his credit Fr. Peyramale as a Parish Priest had to tread cautiously. However, he came to believe that it was the Mother of Jesus appearing to Bernadette the moment she came running from the grotto and breathlessly blurted out what the Lady had revealed to her: **"I am the Immaculate Conception."** He realised that the illiterate Bernadette Soubirous had no idea of the monumental significance of what she had just said.

I am the vine and you are the branches. Those who remain in me, and I in them will bear much fruit; for you can do nothing without me.

In preaching devotion to Mary DeMontfort stressed the supreme importance of being faithful to one's baptismal promises. In that light the primary meaning of the yellow roses growing on Mary's feet can be found in John's gospel chapter 15:5: *"I am the vine and you are the branches. Those who remain in me, and I in them will bear much fruit; for you can do nothing without me"*. We are alive in Christ; we grow in Him on the Mystical Vine. Our Lady is challenging us to rise above the imperfect status of a lukewarm a la carte Christianity; that is to say, the precarious state of being neither hot nor cold. It is a timely warning echoing Revelation 3:15-16 *"I know about your activities: how you are neither hot nor cold, I wish you were one of the other. But since you are neither hot nor cold, but only lukewarm, I will spit you out of my mouth."* Being a practising Catholic means to be a follower of Christ in the full sense of the word.

Therefore intimacy with Our Lady ought to lead us to full sacramental communion with Jesus Christ. There is no middle ground in the spiritual order. Either one is hot getting hotter, or one is lukewarm growing colder, that's the stark reality Christians must face up to.

Humpty Dumpty had a great fall

Foremost in the mind of Frank Duff was the thought that Jesus loved him personally and that 'The Passion of Jesus is a work of Infinite Love.'[15] Humanity like 'Humpty Dumpty' had a great fall and all the Kings horses and all the Kings men, couldn't put Humpty Dumpty together again', that is to say, no cosmic power or human agency could ever restore humanity to wholeness. Paradoxically, only in the brokenness of Jesus Christ on the Cross can each person be 'put back together again'. Like the Israelite's in the desert bitten by the fiery serpents we too are obliged to look to Christ Crucified.[16] Mary teaches us that the Cross is our only hope.[17] It is the shadow of the Cross that reassures mankind that Light exists; if there is no light there can be no shadow. Without the Cross we would still be held in the 'Powers' of Darkness, still guilty, fatally contaminated. Only in the Son of God hanging on the Cross of Calvary are we deemed 'Not guilty.'[18] The Cross is interwoven into the fabric of human existence.

---

[15] St Paul of the Cross.
[16] The Book of Numbers 21:4-9
[17] John 12:23
[18] See Romans chapter 5

By means of the cross the Baptised are free to make the Passover to the 'next' by threading 'dry shod' through the waters of earthly life to eternal life.

This day you will be with me in Paradise

When Our Lady of Lourdes addressed Bernadette "I do not promise to make you happy in this world, but in the next." She was echoing the Saviour's pledge to the 'Good Thief', *"This day you will be with me in paradise."* Like St John, little Bernadette is representative of all contrite hearts open to accept God's free gift of eternal life. The Cross, the 'Tree of Life' stands in the mystical garden of Mt. Calvary where God definitively addressed humankind through His only Son Jesus Christ, the 'New Adam,' in the presence of Mary the 'Woman of Genesis' *"This day you will be with me in Paradise".* Satan, knowing that the Blood of the Lamb had defeated him and that access to the 'Tree of Life' is no longer closed to mankind fled in defeat. *"The great winged creatures guarding the tree of life*[19] in the Garden of Eden began preening their feathers in preparation for flight as their mission on earth had come to an end. O happy day! Once again Yahweh may be seen strolling through the golden fields of immortality 'in the cool of the day'[20] and the New Eve, Mother of the living is empowered by God to stretches forth her mighty arm of maternal protection over each one of her

---

[19] Genesis 3:24
[20] Genesis 3:8

spiritual children and make this solemn pledge: "I do not promise to make you happy in this world, but in the next." Through Baptism we have already entered into the happiness of the 'next', the state of heaven all the way to heaven. Our Lady did not use the word 'Heaven', instead she used the word 'next' to indicate that among the thorns and thistles of life, there is the capacity in every human heart to be truly interiorly happy like St Bernadette; a happiness that transcends all shades of earthly happiness.

The man who makes the Holy Spirit his helper enters into the tide of omnipotence

"The Spirit we have received is not the spirit of the world, but God's own Spirit, so that we may understand the lavish gifts God has given us."[21] Our Lady draws souls away from the 'spirit of the world' to be open to the Holy Spirit in loving aware of God's omnipotence every moment of our lives. Frank Duff was very aware of this reality for he wrote in the handbook: "The man who makes the Holy Spirit his helper enters into the tide of omnipotence."[22] Accordingly, each soul rides on the tide of God's omnipotence and is thereby washed onto the shores of the eternal now. True devotion means loving Jesus and Mary moment to moment with all its consequences and being aware of the Holy Spirit within.

---

[21] 1 Corinthians 2:12
[22] Handbook page 44

When Frank Duff initially made his own request to be in filled with the Holy Spirit and to live within the confluence of love that existed between the Spirit and Our Lady, he must have felt like Alice in wonderland.[23] One moment he was looking down at a tiny door that seemed impossible for him to enter, being blocked by time, distance and proportion. However, just like Alice in wonderland, he began to shrink to the scale of the miniature door that opens the way to the secret garden of mystical union with Our Lady. When that happens one becomes rooted in the 'Sacrament of the present moment' whereby 'amid the crosses, toils and disappointments of life' we continuously surrender our will to God's will. Day after day, night after night, moment to moment we give our 'Fiat' to God. That's the greatest response an individual can give to God and it's the secret of interior equilibrium and happiness; the antithesis of the current pessimistic rise of Existentialism. Since the powers of the soul do not extent beyond the boundary of the present moment we may expect 'the Divine Assistance to remain always with us'. What a joy it is to realise that Paradise dwells within and that we are never separated from the 'All Presence' of God, not even for a second. Therefore we may say that the Sacrament of the present moment is the

---

[23] The Legionary Promise on page 90 of the Legion of Mary Handbook. Printed at the back of this book

fountain of 'eternal youth', the trysting well of all mystics; that is to say, all those who thirst for God.

Joy is the calling card of the Holy Spirit and it penetrates through the permafrost of the subconscious, filling the soul with certitude that the Kingdom of God is within. The great Doctor of the Church, St Therese of the Child Jesus grasped this truth very early in life: "I don't know what I shall do in heaven, I shall be with God, but I can't think what it will be like, because I am already there entirely with Him on earth." Therese is not referring to extraordinary graces or mystical abstractions from conscious reality; she is talking about the ordinary circumstances in which she experienced the presence of God. Yes, we find Jesus hidden in the Sacred Bread, the Eucharist, but we ought to be constantly aware of the Holy Spirit hidden in the sacrament of the presence moment. After long searching St. Augustine discovered God's presence within and he exclaimed in his Confessions: "Late have I loved you, O Beauty so ancient and so new; late have I loved you! For behold you were within me, and I outside". Such is the condescension of this 'Tremendous Lover' that He is forced to go outside to knock on the door of our consciousness in order to make us aware that He lives within us in the nanoseconds of the 'next'. *Where shall I go to escape your spirit? Where shall I flee from your presence? If I scale the heavens you are there, if I lie in Sheol, there you are.'* (Psalm 139 v7)

Make the wild roses bloom

It's important for all Christians to know that Our Lady at Lourdes appeared at a perilous time in history when ruinous secular ideologies were fermenting in sick minds and about to be unleashed across the globe; as a result millions would die and untold numbers would lose their faith. Seen today against the backdrop of aggressive atheism and secularism, Fr. Peyramale' request "Make the wild roses bloom" carries with it an urgent appeal to each individual. Paradoxically each individual has the power of will to perform that miracle. All it takes is a simple act of free will to graft ourselves on to the Mystical rose tree– **"I am all yours my Queen and Mother, and all that I have is yours."** Sadly, very few understand that Heaven's call to consecration to the Immaculate Heart of Mary is far more important than we could ever possibly imagine.

Our yes to Mary is always an unequivocal yes to God

People have always accused Catholics of giving too much attention to Mary. The reality is that Catholics have always known that a Mariology without an intimate relationship with Jesus Christ would soon evanesce into Mariolatry. Every Christian ought to know that our yes to Mary is always an unequivocal yes to God; an echo you might say of Mary's yes to God on behalf of humanity.

Blessed John Henry Newman wrote,[24] "The Prophet says, *"There shall come forth a rod out of the root of Jesse, and a flower shall rise out of his root."* Who is the flower but our Blessed Lord? Who is the rod, or beautiful stalk or stem or plant out of which the flower grows, but Mary, Mother of our Lord, Mary, Mother of God?" Hence, we can truly say, to flower in Mary, is to flower in Jesus Christ.

---

[24] 'Blessed Art Thou Among Women' Meditations on Mary by John Henry Cardinal Newman – Introduction

Founder of the Legion of Mary

Chapter 7

Part One

"The maternal duty of Mary toward men in no way obscures or diminishes this unique mediation of Christ, but rather shows its power. All her saving influence on men originates not from some inner necessary, but from the divine pleasure. It flows forth from the superabundance of the merits of Christ, rests on His mediation, depends entirely on it and draws all its power for it." - Vatican II Lumen Gentium: 60, 67)

The Legion of Mary was in existence 30 years before I was born. I entered when I was about 18 years of age. I was 'recruited' by Miss Christina Moynihan and was fortunate that my first President was Miss Marylyn Landers. Like Frank Duff she was a retired civil servant. She had done sterling work as a Legion envoy in Africa. At that particular time, the Legion filled a vacuum in my spiritual life after I returned home from a two year stay with the Passionist Fathers, as a Lay Brother, in North England. Marylyn was an exceptional person who took no prisoners, so to speak; she knocked the cobwebs off me in jig time. I owe so much to this amazing taskmistress. In the spiritual order, Miss bossy boots, as I affectionately called her, was a mover and shaker who believed there is no inferiority in Christ. By that I mean she passionately believed by virtue of Baptism every

Christian has their part to play in building up the Mystical Body of Christ. What a blessing to have found myself under her command. She never shrank from her task of forming new apostles. Like the great Frank Duff, she saw the D.N.A. of a saint in everybody. Not everybody liked her methods but I have no doubt that Marylyn Landers dispensed to me the correct medicine to grow in Christ at that particular time of my life. This exceptional woman was one of a new breed of warrior saint that came off the production line of the Legion of Mary. The best compliment I could pay Marylyn is that Frank Duff, Founder of the Legion of Mary was fond of her.

Torremolino

It was Marylyn's bright idea to arrange a meeting for me and my fiancé with Frank Duff in 1976. During that intimate meeting he spoke to me very convincingly about Angels and he even ventured to guess a name for my guardian angel. He leaned back in his chair and thought for a minute and then as if someone had whispered into his ear he suddenly said, "Torremolino!" Frank had no idea that Anne and I intended to spend our honeymoon in Torremolinos in the south of Spain. When I pointed this out to him he triumphantly exclaimed with a big smile, "There you are!"

"God sent His Angels."

By way of encouraging me to start writing he spoke of a legionary who wrote an inspiring article about Angels, emphasising that she had no theological training. I got a keen sense that he was familiar with Angels. Later I became convinced he had a visit from an Angel sent by God to administer to him the apostolic flame that constituted him for sure, not only founder of the Legion of Mary, but Father of the Lay Apostolate. He seemed to be captivated by the recurring item in the bible *"God sent His Angels."* According to his reckoning "there are about 300 references to the Angels in the two testaments." In his article 'The Angels' he wrote, "St. Bernard insists that it is of paramount necessity that we should have a positive devotion to the Angels. So great is their office in regard to us that it must be repaid by the bestowing of some attention on them."[1] He regarded the Annunciation[2] as the centre point of Legionary devotion and he recognised the Angel Gabriel as a protector not only of Mary but of each of Mary's children. Therefore the Archangel Gabriel holds a special place of honour in the Legion of Mary.

Chosen and empowered by God

It seems not everyone regards Frank Duff as 'Founder' of the Legion of Mary. Some years ago I had a conversation with a nun who emphatically maintained that he was not the founder of the Legion. She did however consider him a co-founder. Of course I disagreed with her. I feel certain that Frank would have sided with the reverent Sister. I then began thinking of ways to convince her and every other person who did not consider him the authentic founder of the Legion. Then in Lourdes some time later I came across a book written by Guy Gaucher, Auxiliary Bishop of Bayeux and

---

[1] Mary Shall Reign – chapter 21
[2] See CCC969

Lisieux entitled "John and Therese: Flames of Love."[3] That book pointed me in the right direction. It filled me with certitude that Frank Duff had supernatural backing and that he was chosen and empowered by God for the task he so faithfully carried out with such élan and pragmatic efficiency.

Charismatically equipped

To assist him in his mission he received from on high the gift of Transverberation, more commonly known as the 'Wound of love'. I am not implying that he was more virtuous than others. I am implying however, that he did not rise entirely on his own merits and abilities to gain the title founder of the legion. The Holy Spirit had singled him out and was with him in his undertakings; it was the grace of the wound of love that charismatically gave him his seal of office, thus separating and equipping him as the authentic founder of the Legion of Mary.

Prime mover and shaker

It made perfect sense to me and explained why he among others became the Legion's prime mover and shaker. Nevertheless, I realised I would have my work cut out to explain my personal conviction to the good nun or to anybody else for that matter. Therefore with the help of Bishop Gaucher's book and the writings of the Carmelite mystics and a dose of my own arrogance I will attempt to

---

[3] John and Therese: Flames of Love – (The influence of St John of the Cross in the Life of St. Therese of Lisieux) St Pauls, Alba House – New York. It first appeared in 1999.

justify my hypothesis regarding Frank Duff's receiving the wound of Love.

Did not our hearts burn within us?

We are all familiar with Gian Lorenzo Bernini's sculpture of the classic image of the Transverberation of St Teresa of Avila. It depicts an Angel with an arrow tipped with fire wounding the heart of the Saint; Transverberation is the technical name for the mystical wound of love. Let's start with explaining what it is not. The experience of heat glowing in around the heart area is quite a common spiritual experience. I have met people who have experienced this type of phenomena. At times the heart heats up. Sometimes it may become so alarmingly hot that any jewellery such as chains or medals resting over the heart area actually heat up to the point of physically burning the skin beneath. The gospels mention this phenomenon when the two disciples met Jesus on the road to Emmaus. *"Did not our hearts burn within us as he talked to us on the road and explained the scriptures to us?"*[4] However, this burning of the heart ought not to be confused with the fiery wound of love which can be compared to an anointing by the Holy Spirit. One may say it replaces the horn of oil that the prophets used in the Old Testament. In transverberation an Angel is sent by God to anoint with the taper of fire from Heaven just as Samuel was sent to anoint David with holy oil. Anointing with oil or fire are both forms of empowerment signifying a type of power sharing with

---

[4] Luke 24:32

the Holy Spirit; *and the spirit of the Lord came mightily upon David from that day forward.* [5]

A fiery dart

From the autobiographical writings of St John of the Cross, particularly his book 'The Living Flame of Love' one can deduce some outstanding features that distinguish the charismatic grace of transverberation from the more common mystical burning of the heart. Firstly, this mystical wound of the spirit registers sensibly in the heart and John of the Cross and Teresa of Avila both speak of an Angel with a fiery dart.[6]

Secondly, when the Angel strikes the blow registers in the sensible part of one's nature, as if struck with force by something like a long wooden handle.

Thirdly, the flame burns sensibly just as a lighted match would burn the skin if applied to it, hence, John of the Cross described this inner fire as a 'Living Flame.' Although according to him the sharp pain is greatly assuaged by a potent admixture of joy and exhilaration. It is perhaps the greatest physical proof of the existing of God.

Fourthly, transverberation has the distinction of taking a soul to the precipice of death. If the flame did not cease to burn, death would immediately ensue. It's important to point out that Therese of Lisieux was already on fire

---

[5] 1 Samuel 16:13

[6] "In his hands I saw a long golden spear and at the end of the iron tip I seemed to see a point of fire." St Teresa of Avila

with love for God prior to the grace of transverberation, as was the case with John of the cross, Teresa of Avila and indeed St Francis of Assisi. As the flame abruptly extinguishes one continues to be on fire with love for God, yet it cannot be denied that this charismatic grace stokes the flames of love for God in the recipient and leave a metaphysical wound of love in the soul and sometimes, as St John of the cross tells us, this inner wound sometimes registers in the flesh as stigmata. However, the point I wish to highlight here is that, at no stage do we get a sense that the two disciples on the road to Emmaus considered that their lives were suddenly about to end by the sensible burning feeling of their hearts; that fiery glow did not threaten their mortality.

Oh! What fire and what sweetness at one and the same time!

Two years before her death St Therese of the Child Jesus experienced this mystical wound when she was praying the Stations of the Cross[7] She explains; "I was seized with such a violent love for God that I can't explain it except by saying I felt as though I was totally plunged into fire. Oh! What fire and what sweetness at one and the same time! I was on fire with love, and I felt that one minute, one second more and I wouldn't be able to sustain this ardour without dying."

Few persons have reached these heights

What's important for me is the discovery Bishop Gaucher made in respect of this phenomenon from the writings of Fr. Marie Eugene. On page 123 of his book,

---

[7] This happened at the fourth station where Jesus meets His mother.

the Carmelite Bishop quotes Fr. Marie-Eugene of the Child Jesus, an expert on Carmelite Spirituality. "He asks what is all this about? The answer is given to us by St John of the cross, who accompanied St Teresa of Jesus on some of her journeys: **"Few persons have reached these heights. Some have, however, especially those whose virtue and spirit were to be diffused among their children. With respect to the first fruits of the spirit, God accords to Founders wealth and value commensurate with the greater or lesser following they will have in their doctrine and spirituality"**[8]

Apostolic flame

Bishop Gaucher goes on to say: "I owe to Fr. Marie-Eugene of the Child Jesus the discovery of the meaning of this event (wound of love) in Therese's life in 1895." Fr. Marie Eugene comments: "At the fourth station of her Way of the Cross, she receives a wound of love that elevates her for sure (she was probably already there) to the transforming union, which is a wound of spiritual motherhood that we can probably compare to the transverberation of St Teresa (Avila) and which will give her the mission of disseminating her knowledge of God. She will therefore take this knowledge of love as her departure point in order to transmit her doctrine of spiritual childhood." Do you see where I am going with this line of thought? What Fr. Marie-Eugene said about St Therese and Teresa of Avila may equally be said of the Founder of the Legion of Mary and his apostolic mission.

---

[8] See The Living Flame of Love written by St. John of the Cross.

While writing this book it occurred to me the probability that Our Blessed Lady passed into eternal life by the action of a high ranking Angel sent to administer to her the ultimate wound of love that instantly ended her earthly existence before assuming her incorrupt body and soul into Glory. With the ecstatic preliminaries of her reunion with her Divine Son over, Mary continues in her glorified condition to exercises her God given Motherhood of the Mystical Body of Christ, that is to say each member of it. Paradoxically, Our Lady's 'Yes' to God (*"Let it be done to me according to your word"*[9] produced the initial spark that ignited humanity in the fires of Trinitarian Love. Through Mary mankind is destined to burn forever in the fires of Merciful Love! It seems right and fitting that the Blessed Mother of the Saviour should pass into glory by the same Flame of Merciful Love that entered her at the moment of the Incarnation.

It is to your advantage that I go away

The 'tongues of fire' resting over the heads of the Apostles and Our Lady was an outward manifestation of the fiery DNA of eternal life in Jesus Christ burning within them. Later the Apostles understood the words of Jesus; *"It is to your advantage that I go away"* [10]In the New Adam (Jesus) man is born again by the water of baptism and the fire of the Spirit. In this we glimpse the New Eve's (Mary) unique status – her Motherhood of

---

[9] Luke 1:38
[10] John 16:7

the God-Man and her simultaneous Motherhood of the mystical extension of Christ's Body, the Church. It was Frank Duff's clear understanding of the doctrine of the Mystical Body that bound him so intimately with the Holy Spirit and Our Lady.

Lighting a candle

Let us come back to the mystical wound of love. It seems to me that one may compare it to a person who goes into a church and lights a candle. The lighted candle becomes an outward physical manifestation of the person's interior wish or intention; the wound of love is something of that kind. It is an interior manifestation of the Holy Spirits intention for that particular individual and consequently brings with it *strength to his right arm*. In other words the Spirit gives empowerment to the chosen person to carry out His particular mission in the Mystical Body of Christ. It is therefore an apostolic flame directed to the good of the whole Church. Filled with the Holy Spirit's intention the individual becomes a lighted candle, a flaming Cross, or as DeMontfort prophetically said, "Ministers of the Lord who, like a burning fire, shall kindle the fire of divine love everywhere." (TD56) That description of DeMontfort most certainly fits Frank Duff. Just as one would touch the naked flame of a candle to light up another one; that's the way a charism works. Making contact with the Servant of God, Frank Duff we too become ignited with the same apostolic charism/flame.

It is true that the person receiving this grace may not immediately grasp the Spirit's intention at the time; the person may even be thrown into confusion. Nevertheless, the Holy Spirit gradually enlightens the individual as to their supernatural mission. Just like the design of a new building begins to take shape in the mind of an architect, so too, a grand design began to take shape in the mind of a young Francis Duff. He sees the vast untapped resource of the living stones of the laity scattered about. Like his namesake St Francis of Assisi, responding to God's call, he sets about shaping these living stones into a Gothic masterpiece, so to speak. As the word Gothic suggests he fixes their gaze on higher things. Soon these new Franciscans begin to blossom on the mystical vine. They swell the ranks of *'the few'* lay labourers gathering in the harvest. In a flash of illumination Frank calls this new order of Franciscans, if you will, the Legion of Mary and from the pulpit of his gothic cathedral he preaches that Legionary service is justifiably based on the doctrine of the Mystical Body.'[11]He is on solid theological ground.

The scent of anointing oil exudes from him

One does not wish in any way to minimise the providential role those zealous pioneer members played in the formation of the Legion of Mary. Nevertheless, taking all things into consideration few people fully informed would deny the title 'Founder' universally

---

[11] See Legion handbook, chapter 9 'The Legionary and the Mystical Body of Christ.'

conferred on Frank Duff, given that from the very first meeting "until his death, November 7, 1980, he guided the world wide extension of the Legion with heroic dedication". Furthermore, without him the Legion would not exist today, as we know it. It appears irrefutable that the Holy Spirit ordained him as the rock on which the Legion is built - the scent of anointing oil exudes from him. On that faithful evening on the 7th of September 1921, the eve of Our Lady's Birthday, the scene was providentially set. All heaven's eyes were on the young Francis who walked into Myra House and into Church history, taking his place among a small band of lay apostolically minded people and Fr. Michael Toher. With the rock set in place, the power of the Holy Spirit rested on them. The Queen of Heaven took charge; the Angels began to drum and the embryonic Legion of Mary set pace to conquer the world for Christ. Its method is refreshingly simple, "The Legion aims to bring Mary to the world as the infallible means of winning the world to Jesus"[12]

A charism may be compared to a flame

As Christ had singled Peter out for his great mission, so too, Frank Duff was called to a particular work of Divine Providence in the life of the Church. As stated above a charism may be compared to a flame and anyone who comes into contact with it will be set alight or at least warmed by its heat. So too, his Charism would be transmitted to all who came in touch with him, either by prayer of intersession, reading his books or studying the Legion handbook. In particular, all those heroic members

---

[12] Legion H. B page 25 chapter 6

of the Legion of Mary engaged in the apostolate throughout the world. I have no doubt Mother Church, who is quick to recognise great sanctity in her children, will in due course place him among the elite group of canonised founders of religious institutions; all those elected by the Holy Spirit to pass on their spiritual wisdom such as the great Saints and Doctors of the Church.

The Legion of Mary without Frank Duff may be compared to a spider without a web.

I reflect again on the words of Cardinal Suenens that prompted this particular series of reflections in the first place: **"Frank Duff is a mystic whose intimate spiritual life deserves to be known some day: it will reveal the depth and the source of his achievements and of his inspiration".** I do not think there was any doubt in the Cardinal's mind that members of the Legion of Mary, Laity, Priests and Religious are to inherit his spirit just as religious Orders such as the Franciscans, Jesuits, Dominicans, Carmelites, Passionists etc. have inherited the particular charism of their respective founders. It is Duff's apostolic spirit that permeates this world-wide organization and any deviation from the spirit of its founder would compromise the Legion's authentic status within the Catholic Church. The Legion of Mary without Frank Duff may be compared to a spider without a web. Nevertheless the Legion does not have exclusivity on him, no more than the Franciscans, Jesuits, Dominicans and Passionists may exercise copyright, so to speak, on their holy founders. Like them Frank Duff is the property of the Church, the people of God.

Founder of the
Legion of Mary

Part Two

For Frank Duff true devotion to Mary meant a true concern for the spiritual welfare of each person, true devotion to the nation and to the whole world. He saw the world through the lens of the Catholic Church as a "people made one with the unity of the Father and Son and Holy Spirit."[13] In a way he has in effect established true Catholic identity among the laity in the life of the Church. He explodes the myth that mystics are those who disengage themselves from the world in order to commune with God. His deep prayer life in no way abstracted him from people or his surroundings. On the contrary, he enthusiastically embraced life and drank the chalice of life to the dregs. Not only that, but he strove to improve it for others in the best possible way, namely, by establishing the 'Reign of Christ' in every human being.

This man is very good

One wonders that if Frank Duff had not been led by divine providence to embrace the particular life he so generously lived, would he have become a Priest. Certainly, the priesthood would have suited his admirable spirit of self-sacrifice, his extraordinary

---

[13] Lumen Gentium Chapter 1 section 4

dedication to the recitation of the Divine Office, love of the Eucharist, his knowledge of Sacred Scripture and his profound understanding of the Mystical Body of Christ. His love of the Mass was matched by his great respect for the dignity of the Catholic Priesthood. Indeed, many Priests and laity came to seek his guidance. Many of those who came to consult him had a sense of awe when he came towards them. At Legion headquarters I witnessed a German Priest waiting to speak to Mr Duff. Like an excited school boy, he kept repeating in a strong guttural accent to his companion "This man is very good … this man is very good." When Frank appeared armed with his fountain pen, he instinctively stood to attention as if the Pope had just walked in. Needless to say he had Mr Duff's full attention.

Mt Alvernia

Implicit in true devotion to Our Lady is a true love for the Eucharist. Michael Francis Duff is that great luminous sign pointing to the Eucharist. One invariably thinks of the vision of St John Bosco of the Church as the Bark of Peter under attack from flotillas of opposing ideologies, while being anchored to the Eucharist and the Blessed Virgin Mary. No one who knew him could dispute the fact that his life was deeply rooted in the Eucharist. In fact his life can be described as intensely Eucharistic. For him the Eucharist was his daily fix, his 'Damascus' encounter, his 'Mt Alvernia' whereby he drew all his spiritual energy. He wrote in the Legion handbook, "The Mass contains everything that Christ offered to God, and all that he acquired for men; and the offerings of those who assist at Mass becomes one with the great offering of Christ."[14]

The Mass is a trilling adventure

He craved the Bread of Life as an addict craves heroine. One can understand why he described the Mass as "a trilling adventure." [15] He seemed to be uncommonly sensitive to the presence of Jesus in the Eucharist. It seems at the solemn moment of the Consecration he was transported in spirit beyond the threshold of bodily experience to Calvary itself, to the place where the riddle of human existence is permanently resolved. There to die mystically with Jesus on the Cross and simultaneously to feel the metaphysical rush of His Resurrection coursing through his spiritual veins. He was present at the miracle of the (Mass) Eucharist every day of his life.

The Eucharist is the keystone of the Catholic system

The Cross of the Resurrection is the ultimate sign of human freedom. "When they see the Son of God lifted up, they will unite themselves to him to be but a single victim for the Mass is their sacrifice as well as his sacrifice." [16] With certitude Frank knew that the Mass and Christ's sacrifice on Calvary are one and the same. In that light he pointed out "The Eucharist is the keystone of the Catholic system."[17] His powerful writings are remarkably consonant with another

---

[14] Handbook chapter 8, 'The Legionary and the Eucharist' page 46
[15] Recommend to read John 6: 22 to 66
[16] Handbook Chapter 8 section - 3 page 48
[17] Mary Shall Reign by Frank Duff – chapter 3 - Capharnaum and the Eucharist, page 30

practitioner of 'True devotion to Mary' Saint Pope John Paul II who expressed himself: "The Church draws her life from the Eucharist." "The Second Vatican Council rightly proclaimed that the Eucharistic sacrifice is "the source and summit of the Christian life." "For the most holy Eucharist contains the Church's entire spiritual wealth: Christ himself, our Passover and living bread. Through his own flesh, now living and life-giving by the Holy Spirit, he offers life to men."[18] If Catholics really understood the Mass and the Eucharist we would have packed Churches and no shortage of good and holy Priests. Jesus Christ would be loved and adored as Lord and Saviour and lives would be ordered to goodness and love of our neighbour.

Redonblue

If asked to describe Frank Duff's spirituality I would describe it in one word, 'Redonblue'. This rather abstract term is my own homespun catchword aimed at emphasising the powerful synergy of Pneumatology and Mariology that was a salient feature of his spirituality. He instinctively understood that 'True Devotion to Mary' was tantamount to 'True Devotion to the Holy Spirit'; both mysteriously perfected the other. No points for guessing the colour red stands for Holy Spirit and blue for Mary. In him the prophetic words of St Louis Marie De Montfort became a reality. "The more the Holy Spirit finds Mary, His dear and inseparable spouse, in any soul, the more active and mighty He becomes in producing Jesus Christ in that soul, and that soul in Jesus Christ." The Holy Spirit illumined his mind when he

---

[18] Ecclesia de Eucharistia 1

penned his stupendous 'Legion Promise' prayer that released such power among the rank and file of the Laity. Frank was certain that those who sincerely make their 'Promise' would be led by the Holy Spirit in union with Our Lady. Effectively his apostolic prayer uniquely connects the laity online with Our Lady and the Holy Spirit, so to speak. Consequently, he had a refined sense that Mary's Immaculate Heart was less a place of refuge, rather a battle station to sally forth in the power of the Spirit to conquer the world in the name of Jesus Christ.

His prayer was always marked by the simplicity of a child

Frank stated "The Christian must imitate Christ. So he must bestow on Mary a love which imitates that which Jesus gave her; a devotion not from the heart alone, but from the intellect as well."[19] His dear friend and confidant of 40 years the wonderful Father Francis Ripley informs us; "He was Mary's child and therefore his prayer was always marked by the simplicity of a child."[20] He did not separate the action of the Holy Spirit from the mission of Mary in the Church and those who joined the Legion of Mary had to become Redonblue, that is to say, no one may become an active member unless they formally made their 'Promise' to the Holy Spirit which bound them to the maternal mission of Mary in the 'penultimate reality' of earthly life. In addition, Legionaries are required to attend the annual ceremony called the Acies – a formal act of submission to the Blessed Virgin in which each Legionary

---

[19] Frank Duff – article 'The Legion is pure Christocentrism'. (Virgo Praedicanda)
[20] A Memoir by Francis J. Ripley page 11

proclaims; "I am all yours my Queen and mother and all that I have is yours".[21]

His loyalty to the Magisterium was absolute

I do not like the term Marian Mystic because it suggests to some that one is not entirely Christ centred. Indeed, Frank was a Christ-centred man. He radiated Christ and saw Christ in his fellow human beings. His mystical life orbited around Jesus Christ who was the supreme love of his heart. For him being Christocentric was not a mere pointing towards Christ, rather it meant a conscientious living in Him and then an outward radiating of Him.[22] He did not make a vow of poverty, chastity and obedience but he lived with great simplicity as though he had; he was a joyful person. In all things he saw the need to be contingent on the reception of the Sacraments of the Church. His loyalty to the Magisterium, which had the authority of Christ, was absolute; he would not place his big toe one inch beyond its jurisdiction. In this he excites loyalty to the magisterium in every member of the Legion of Mary.

A jigsaw puzzle

By no means was he a fanatical Catholic. Like Blessed John Henry Cardinal Newman, he acknowledged the Catholic Church to be the custodian of 360 degrees of revealed Truth. From this panorama he saw the various fragments of truth scattered about and he wanted to piece

---

[21] Legion of Mary handbook Chapter 30 page 173 The Acies
[22] The Woman of Genesis by Frank Duff article' The Legion is pure Christocentrism' page 215

them all together as a child would piece together a jigsaw puzzle. Only then could one appreciate the sheer brilliance of the masterpiece of the Holy Spirit that is the one true Church founded by Christ. It is a matter of public record that he worked for Christian unity during most of his life. He wrote "Make no mistake about it. The faith must be brought to the notice of persons outside the Church. Timidity and human respect and difficulties of one kind and another must all be swallowed up in the supreme desire to share the gift of faith with those who have it not. The Gospel must be brought to every creature."[23]

A man who has spent far too long in the Garden of Gethsemane

Intellectually gifted, a great communicator and writer, Frank had a way with people. Yet he was not a crowd pulling dynamic speaker, nor did he stand out in a crowd. However, neither did some of the great saints, such as St John Vianney, known as the Cure de Ars, the jewel in the crown of the Catholic Priesthood. Frank Duff, the Jewel in the crown of the Royal Priesthood of the Laity, like the holy Cure became a luminous 'Signpost' for others. Filled with zeal for the salvation of souls, he possessed the same Priestly willingness 'to march into Hell for a heavenly cause'; to pass through terrifying caverns of darkness, to experience interior abandonment in union with the Heart of Christ. Whenever I look into the eyes of that melancholy photo of Mr Duff on the cover of Father Boniface Hanley's booklet 'Frank Duff - one of the best' I see an Ecce

---

[23] Frank Duff, A memoir by Canon Francis J Ripley page 12

Homo[24], I see a mystic who had spent far too long in the Garden of Gethsemane.

God wills you to be holy

For the Servant of God it was irrelevant if one was a big flower or a little flower, a little saint of a big saint; all draw their sustenance from the same Holy Spirit: *"We are members of His Body."*[25] Like the essence of an acorn is to grow into an oak tree, he believed and his writings reflect that each Christian is destined to become a saint. As the word 'Music' incorporates all varieties from vibrant Mariachi to the elegant waltz music of Johann Strauss, so too, the word 'Saint" encapsulates all shades of holiness. To become holy requires our willingness to enter into partnership with the Holy Spirit. The sister of St. Thomas Aquinas one day asked him what she must do to become a saint. "Velle" he replied – i.e. "Will it." Why must we will it? St Paul provides the answer, *"God wills you to be holy."*[26] *"Thus he chose us in Christ before the world was made to be holy and faultless."*[27] St Peter also instructs, *'Be yourselves holy in all your activity, after the model of the Holy One who calls us', since scripture says, 'Be holy, for I am holy'.*[28] Frank Duff taught that holiness was best realised under the motherly guidance of Our Lady.

---

[24] John 19:5
[25] Eph 5:30
[26] 1 Thessalonians 4:3
[27] Ephesians 1:4
[28] 1 Peter 1:15 -16

It sparkles with holy unction

The Legion handbook written by Mr Duff and cherished by Legionaries all over the world contains the precious knowledge of the way that God conducts his affairs with His people and demonstrates Christianity in praxis. Although the handbook is replete with basic rules and guidelines it sparkles with holy unction and no matter how many times one reads it, one discovers new seams of enlightenment, new gems of wisdom. It is par excellence a practical guide to True devotion to Mary and ought to be read by all right minded Christians. One thing is certain that anyone who reads it will be challenged to commit themselves to Christ in Catholic action in one form or another. In addition one will see the need to acknowledge the action of the Holy Spirit and enter into a loving relationship with Him.

Swept him along in its current

The Legionary Promise[29] is perhaps the interpretive key to Frank Duff's mystical life: **"Let your power overshadow me, and come into my soul with fire and love and make it one with Mary's love and Mary's will to save the world"**[30] Many have written splendidly about the Holy Spirit and the Blessed Virgin Mary but they seldom stressed the nexus between them; Frank did just that. His love and devotion to the Holy Spirit and Our Lady formed one mighty torrent that swept him along in its current. Yet his 'Redonblue' spirituality is not something new, rather, it is impeccable Catholicism.

---

[29] Attached to this article

[30] The Legion of Mary Promise written by Frank Duff - HB chapter 15: see back of this book.

Like the Catholic Church he looked to Mary as an Icon of eschatological freedom; she is fully human and fully alive in glory with full powers to enter in and out of time to assist us. Unfortunately, many Christians do not see Mary in that light. They are like people looking at the huge figure of the Statue of Liberty and yet fail to grasp the concept of liberty that the statue represents. Yet a few quiet moments of mental adjustment while looking at the Statue would give people a true theological profile of Our Lady. Her right arm boldly holds out the 'Living Flame' the Holy Spirit. In her left hand she holds the Bible, the Word of God, Jesus Christ, Saviour of the World. The seven prong crown is representative of the Church and her seven Sacraments whereby grace flows out upon humanity from the Heart of Christ. Her feet rest triumphantly upon the broken chains that once bound humanity in slavery to Satan. Mary, the New Eve, Mother to the living stands foursquare on the 'one holy and apostolic Catholic Church' founded by Jesus Christ.

Life in the Spirit means living in the eternal now

In the order of nature we walk before we run, so too in a spiritual sense; by walking with Mary we learn to run with her. Here I am using the word running as a metaphor denoting intimacy. In intimacy with Mary Frank Duff lived for the salvation of others and like Mary he was entirely open to the action of the Holy Spirit. Without the divine Pneuma (Holy Spirit) filling our sails, so to speak, we are in danger of becoming adrift in the doldrums of mediocrity. Oftentimes it is just that we are ignorant of the presence of the Holy Spirit in our own lives. One of the positives of 'True Devotion to

Mary' is that Our Lady fans the flame of love for this most Adorable third Person of the Blessed Trinity. Mary makes us aware of the relationship that exists between the Holy Spirit and ourselves, especially in the work of salvation. In the company of Our Lady we will learn to sit quietly amid the secluded woodlands of the eternal now to experience the gentle stirrings of the 'Awesome one'[31] within. 'Hast thou not heard his silent steps? He comes, comes, ever comes[32].' like the calming sound of a babbling spring the Holy Spirit tiptoes majestically through our faculties with the greatest of ease only to leave the human heart palpitating in restless wonder.

Mary leads us to the Holy Spirit

Fr. Thomas O'Flynn C.M. in his book 'Frank Duff, as I knew him' relates that 'Cardinal Suenens points out that the Legion was the first setting in modern times for the popular devotion to the Holy Spirit'. [33] Cardinal Leon Joseph Suenens who was involved with the Catholic Charismatic Renewal Movement had a great admiration for Frank Duff and the Legion of Mary. He was so impressed with his elevated prayer (The Promise) that he wrote a book about it entitled, "Theology of the Apostolate of the Legion of Mary" In it he echoes Frank's conviction, "Mary leads us to the Holy Spirit to know Him and to love Him." Frank was delighted with the Cardinal's book and he wrote in the Legion handbook: "This invaluable work should be read by every responsible Catholic, for it contains a remarkable

---

[31] Psalm 76:11

[32] Tagore: from preface of The Hound of Heaven by Francis Thompson

[33] Praedicanda Publications first published by in 1981 - reprinted in 2007 by Mahons Printing works, Dublin 1

exposition of the principles which governs the Christian apostolate." It mentions also: "It is significant that the first corporate act of the Legion of Mary was to address itself to the Holy Ghost by His invocation and prayer and then proceeding by the rosary to Mary and her Son."[34]

The Legion of Mary is the definitive answer to Frank's question 'Can we be Saints?

When Frank wrote 'Can we be Saints?' he was unaware of the paradigm shift that was taking place in the area of Marian devotion. At the same time he was not aware that the Divine Providence had actually chosen him to be instrumental in establishing 'True Devotion to Mary' among the vast populous of the laity. In union with Our Lady he set up a Saint manufacturing plant so to speak, producing saints of all shapes and sizes; mobilising a vast Legion to assist Priests and patrol the margins of the world in pursuit of the lost sheep. He actively engaged the laity in the apostolate long before Vatican II stated: "The burden of spreading the faith according to his abilities weights on every disciple of Christ." [35] As the 'guiding light' of the Legion of Mary, he incorporated De Montfort's Theology into the Legion system. It is an empirical fact that the Legion of Mary is the definitive answer to the question 'Can we be Saints?

The alchemy of union with Mary

Before we move on, it is vital to point out to all those who may be wavering at the call for intimate union with Mary demanded by DeMontfort's 'True Devotion to the

---

[34] Legion of Mary handbook page 41 The Legionary and the Holy Trinity.
[35] Lumen Gentium chapter 2

Blessed Virgin Mary.' "In union there are still two, in unity there is but one."[36] The wonderful alchemy of union with Mary transforms silver into gold, that is to say, it leads to oneness in Jesus Christ. It is rather silly to maintain that union with Mary eclipses unity in Christ. Rather, Mary made unity in Jesus possible by her Fiat in the first place. If that becomes clear in your mind, then the clouds of doubt will instantly disappear and you will have received the grace to understand the true meaning of Consecration to the Immaculate Heart of Mary. To do so is to be free from all impediments to advanced life in the Holy Spirit – or as DeMontfort puts it, to breathe the Holy Spirit.

This devotion consists in giving oneself entirely to Mary in order to belong entirely to Jesus through her.

When we 'breathe the Holy Spirit,' if you will, we breathe in and out eternal life in the sacrament of the present moment. In practical terms this means we have to abdicate the throne and crown Jesus Lord of ourselves and our lives. How can we acclaim Christ as our King otherwise? Frank Duff, the layman's guide to true devotion to Mary advocated the best way of doing this is by means of consecration to Our Lady, to crown her Queen: "By the perfect practise of true devotion to Mary as taught by St. Louis de Montfort summed up by him as follows: "This devotion consists in giving oneself entirely to Mary in order to belong entirely to Jesus through her. It requires us to give:

(1) Our body, with its senses and members;

---

[36] See Letter of St Therese to her sister Celine 'January 1889' in which she makes use of this quotation.

(2) Our soul with its faculties;

(3) Our present material possessions and all we shall acquire in the future;

(4) Our interior and spiritual possessions, that is, our merits, virtues and good actions of the past, the present and the future

In other words we give her all we possess both in our natural life and in our spiritual life as well as everything we shall acquire in the future in the order of nature, of grace and of glory in heaven."[37]

In DeMontfort's other great spiritual classic, 'The Love of Eternal Wisdom' we read: "Here is the great way, the wonderful secret. Let us, so to speak, bring Mary into our abode by consecrating ourselves unreservedly to her as servants and slaves. Let us surrender into her hands all we possess, even what we value most highly, keeping nothing for ourselves. This good Mistress, who never allows herself to be surpassed in generosity will give herself to us in a real but indefinable manner; and it is in her that eternal Wisdom (Jesus Christ) will come and settle as on a throne of splendour."[38]

Mary's motherhood is really an infinite thing

Before we "plunge ourselves into Mary motherhood" there is something every Christian ought to know. Mr Duff explains: 'Mary's motherhood is really an infinite thing, because God has made it part of His own

---

[37] Handbook of the Legion of Mary p340 'Treatise on True Devotion paragraph 121

[38] The Love of Eternal Wisdom' by De Montfort reference 211

parenthood.'[39] In that light Frank wanted all Christians to tap into their Baptismal grace by petitioning the Holy Spirit to enter into a holy alliance with Him. In return the Spirit attaches Himself to our human frailty all the while in complete subjugation to Mary, Mediatrix of all graces. Here I want to introduce a mental picture of Mary's mediation, even if it is an imperfect one. Think of a pyramid of champagne glasses. Only when the first glass is full can all the rest be filled by a continuous pouring into the first glass. Mary is that apex glass, so to speak, which is always full. You will remember that the Angel Gabriel addressed her as "full of grace". Being full of grace Our Lady is in perpetual overflow, that is to say constantly filling the pyramidal assembly of the people of God. In this image we see her as channel or Mediatrix of grace won by her divine Son. You could say the champagne of salvation flows through Mary, as the outstretched hands on the image of the Immaculate Conception suggests.

Without her we cannot know or love you

Union with Mary pivots upon that principle of her spiritual motherhood and mediation of grace. Addressing the Holy Spirit Frank wrote in the Legionary Promise:

"But I know that you, who has come to regenerate the world in Jesus Christ, has not willed to do so except through Mary. That without her we cannot know or love you. That it is by her, and to whom she pleases, when she pleases and in the quantity and manner she pleases; that all your gifts and virtues and graces are

[39] Article by Frank Duff - Have the mind of Mary found in his book 'Woman of genesis'

administered. And I realise that the secret of a perfect legionary service consists in a complete union with her who is so completely united to you."[40]

He urged everyone to "ask for the grace to enter fully into that divine arrangement whereby Mary mothers souls and uses us as helpers."[41]

Journey with Mary to the summit of holiness

His parting gift to me was a signed[42] copy of his book 'Walking with Mary'. Essentially, that's his invitation to everybody; to begin walking with Mary, that is to say, to consecrate our lives to God through Mary, thereby entering into the bottomless reservoir of mystical union with Jesus Christ. In Mary that which we hope for we shall apprehend, and the object of our faith we shall see face to Face. Instinctively Frank Duff knew Our Lady will not accept mediocrity nor allow God's adopted children to remain like the vast majority of Catholics at a makeshift basecamp, content to live their Catholicism on a purely secondary level. He therefore challenges all of us to transcend our subjective attitudes towards our Catholic Faith and fully embrace the Cross of Jesus Christ with all its legitimate objective demands and journey with Mary to the summit of holiness. That is exactly what each member of the Legion of Mary is asked to do, nothing more, nothing less.

---

[40] The Legionary Promise Handbook page 90
[41] Frank Duff's Article – Have the mind of Mary
[42] I asked him to sign it for me.

Mr Duff insisted that "Everyone must pour himself into another soul" and that "We will be called upon to give an account of every soul in the whole world." He knew that the call of Christ must resonate in the heart of every baptised person and that person was called upon to act with God, in God and for God and hence for the salvation of souls. He wrote, "In all those whom they (Legionaries) served they were to see the Person of Jesus Christ himself. This was based upon his understanding of Christ's words: *"Truly, I tell you, just as you did it to one of the least of these who are members of my family, you did it to me."* (Mt 25:40)[43] For Frank Duff these words of Christ found their fulfilment in His exhortation to His Church: "GO PREACH THE GOSPEL TO THE WHOLE CREATION."[44]

Conclusion

"The Church is the sign and instrument of the presence and action of the life –giving Spirit."[45] The resurrection power of the Holy Spirit courses through it veins. Catholicism is the only religion today that stands against all heresies and is the last bastion protecting moral absolutes. In these uncertain times the ark of the Catholic Church is really the safest place to be in. Down through the centuries the various poisonous philosophical winds have failed to extinguish the fires of Pentecost. Enlightened people will observe that the real miracle

---

[43] See Legion handbook chapters 9 and 40

[44] Mark 16:15

[45] (Dominum et Vivificantem 64 - encyclical letter – on the Holy Spirit in the Life of the Church and the world - by Pope John Paul II)

today is that in spite of corruption, mismanagement and some second rate Popes, Bishops, Priests and Lay people, the Catholic Church is alive and kicking. Most importantly as G.K. Chesterton points out, "the Founder of Christianity knows his way out of the grave." It has also something else that no other religion has, namely, the power from Christ to forgive sins. In the future, as in the past, the Church will always have its martyrs, saints and sinners. If the mystical life of Frank Duff has anything to tell us in the 21st Century, it is that nothing can obviate the fact that each person is called by God to eternal life in holiness of life as sons and daughters of the Church and that a true and tender devotion to the Mother of Jesus wonderfully intensifies that reality.

Prayer composed by the Servant of God, Frank Duff

The Legionary Promise

Most Holy Spirit, I, (*name of candidate*),
Desiring to be enrolled this day as a legionary of Mary,
Yet knowing that of myself I cannot render worthy service,
Do ask of you to come upon me and fill me with yourself,
So that my poor acts may be sustained by your power, and
become an instrument of your mighty purposes.

But I know that you who have come to regenerate the world
In Jesus Christ,
Have not willed to do so except through Mary;
That without her we cannot know or love you;
That it is by her, and to whom she pleases, when she pleases,
And in the quantity and manner she pleases,
That all your gifts and virtues and graces are administered;
And I realise that the secret of a perfect legionary service
Consists in a complete union with her who is so completely united
to you.

So, taking in my hand the legionary Standard which seeks to
Set before our eyes these things,
I stand before you as her soldier and her child,
And I so declare my entire dependence on her,
She is the mother of my soul.
Her heart and mind are one
And from that single heart she speaks again those words of old:
"Behold the handmaid of the Lord";
And once again you come by her to do great things.

Let your power overshadow me, and come into my soul with
Fire and love,
And make it one with Mary's love and Mary's will to save the
world;
So that Christ my Lord may likewise grow in me through you:
So that I with her, his Mother, may bring him to the world
And to the souls who need him;
So that they and I, the battle won, may reign with her for ever
in the glory of the Blessed Trinity.

Confident that you will so receive me – and use me – and
turn my weakness into strength this day,
I take my place in the ranks of the Legion, and I venture to
promise a faithful service.
I will submit fully to its discipline,
Which binds me to my comrades,
And shapes us to an army,
And keeps our line as on we march with Mary,
To work your will, to operate your miracles of grace,
Which will renew the face of the earth,
And establish your reign, Most Holy Spirit, over all.
In the name of the Father and the Son and the Holy Spirit, Amen.